PRIVATIZED
PLANET

About the author

TJ Coles is a postdoctoral researcher at Plymouth University's Cognition Institute working on issues relating to blindness and visual impairment. His doctoral thesis *The Knotweed Factor* can be read online.

A columnist with AxisOfLogic, Coles has written about politics and human rights for a number of publications including *CounterPunch, Ethical Space, Newsweek,* the *New Statesman, Peace Review* and *Truthout.*

In 2013, he was shortlisted for the Martha Gellhorn Prize for Journalism for a series of articles about Libya. His books include *Human Wrongs* (iff Books), *Real Fake News* (Red Pill Press), *Union Jackboot* (with Matthew Alford) and *Manufacturing Terrorism* (Clairview Books).

PRIVATIZED PLANET

'FREE TRADE' AS A WEAPON AGAINST DEMOCRACY, HEALTHCARE AND THE ENVIRONMENT

TJ COLES

New Internationalist

Privatized Planet
'Free Trade' as a Weapon Against Democracy,
Healthcare and the Environment

First published in 2019 by
New Internationalist Publications Ltd
The Old Music Hall
106-108 Cowley Road
Oxford
OX4 1JE, UK
newint.org

Design: Juha Sorsa
Cover design: Andrew Kokotka

Printed by T J International Limited, Cornwall, UK
who hold environmental accreditation ISO 14001.

MIX
Paper from
responsible sources
FSC® C013056

British Library Cataloguing-in-Publication Data
A catalogue record for this book is available from the British Library.

Library of Congress Cataloging-in-Publication Data
A catalog record for this book is available from the Library of Congress.

ISBN 978-1-78026-501-8
(ebook ISBN 978-1-78026-502-5)

Contents

Acronyms

ACA	Affordable Care Act
ACEA	European Automobile Manufacturers Association (Association des constructeurs européens d'automobiles)
ACC	American Chemistry Council
AFL-CIO	American Federation of Labor-Congress of Industrial Organizations
AGB	Association of German Banks
APEC	Asia-Pacific Economic Cooperation
ASEAN	Association of Southeast Asian Nations
ASTA	American Seed Trade Association
BIS	Bank for International Settlements
BIT	Bilateral Investment Treaty
BMJ	British Medical Journal
BRIC	Brazil Russia India China
BYOD	bring your own device
CAFTA-DR	Central America-Dominican Republic Free Trade Agreement-
CBI	Confederation of British Industry
CEO	Chief Executive Officer
CEPEA	Comprehensive Economic Partnership for East Asia
CETA	Comprehensive Economic and Trade Agreement (EU-Canada)
CFR	Council on Foreign Relations
CIA	Central Intelligence Agency
CLA	CropLife America
COPINH	Civic Council of Popular and Indigenous Organizations of Honduras
CRS	Congressional Research Service
DES	Diethylstilbestrol
DFID	Department for International Development
DG	Directorate-General (eg for Trade, Environment)
EBF	European Banking Federation
EC	European Commission
ECETOC	European Centre for Ecotoxicology and Toxicology of Chemicals
ECPA	European Crop Protection Association
EDCs	endocrine disrupting chemicals
EEC	European Economic Community
EEU	Eurasian Economic Union
EMU	European Monetary Union
EPA	Environmental Protection Agency
EPRS	European Parliamentary Research Services
ESA	European Seed Association
ESM	European Stability Mechanism
ESR	Electronic Staff Record
EU	European Union
FBI	Federal Bureau of Investigation

FCN	Friendship, Commerce and Navigation (treaty)	MRI	magnetic resonance imaging
FDA	Food and Drug Administration	MRSA	Methicillin-resistant Staphylococcus aureus
FDI	foreign direct investment	NAFTA	North American Free Trade Agreement
FTA	Free Trade Agreement, also Free Trade Area	NASA	National Aeronautics and Space Administration
FTAAP	Free Trade Area of the Asia-Pacific	NATO	North Atlantic Treaty Organization
G8	Group of Eight	NCL	National City Lines
G20	Group of 20	NHS	National Health Service (UK)
GATS	General Agreement on Trade in Services	NTM	non-tariff measure(s)
GATT	General Agreement on Tariffs and Trade	OECD	Organisation for Economic Co-operation and Development
GDP	Gross Domestic Product	
GM	genetically modified	OEEC	Organization for European Economic Co-operation
GMO	genetically modified organism	OEPC	Occidental Exploration and Production Company
GNP	Gross National Product	
HMO	health maintenance organization	OPEC	Organization of Petroleum Exporting Countries
ICC	International Chamber of Commerce	PFI	private finance initiative
ICT	information communication technologies	PRS	public railway services
		PTO	Patent and Trademark Office
IMF	International Monetary Fund	RCEP	Regional Comprehensive Economic Partnership
ISDS	investor-State dispute settlement	REACH	Registration Evaluation Authorisation and Restriction of Chemicals (EU)
ITO	International Trade Organization	
		rBGH	recombinant bovine growth hormone
JEFTA	Japan-EU Free Trade Agreement	SCO	Shanghai Cooperation Organization
LPRI	Lone Pine Resources Inc.	SME	small- to medium-size enterprise
MEP	Member of the European Parliament	SOE	state-owned enterprise
MFN	Most-Favoured Nation	SSM	special safeguard mechanism

TISA	Trade in Services Agreement
TNC	transnational corporation
TPP	Trans-Pacific Partnership
TRIPS	Trade-Related Intellectual Property Rights
TTIP	Transatlantic Trade and Investment Partnership
UN	United Nations
UNCITRAL	United Nations Commission on International Trade Law
UNCTAD	United Nations Conference on Trade and Development
UNEP	United Nations Environmental Programme
USDA	United States Department of Agriculture
USMCA	US-Mexico-Canada Agreement
VAT	value added tax
WEMA	Water Efficient Maize for Africa
WHO	World Health Organization
WTO	World Trade Organization

'This document must be protected
from unauthorized disclosure...
It must be stored in a locked or
secured building, room, or container.'
Trade in Services Agreement,
(Draft) Annex [X]: Financial Services

Introduction

UNITED STATES governments have always put big business first. Despite Donald Trump's unique presidential style, including his shouting about trade wars and protectionist tariffs, the current trajectory of the politics of business has not significantly changed. Profit remains the key motivation and wholesale privatization is one of the consequences. But the means of getting there remain controversial among US elites.

Some favour a 'liberal' world order, in which neat political arrangements that privilege their national businesses, like the Trans-Pacific Partnership (TPP) and the European Union, dominate the global scene. Others prefer 'conservative' bilateralism and more blatant forms of nationalism, like one-on-one 'trade deals' and so-called sovereignty movements such as Brexit. Trump has recently renegotiated one such 'neat' arrangement, the North American Free Trade Agreement (NAFTA) between the US, Mexico and Canada. It is now called the US-Mexico-Canada Agreement (USMCA).[1] And there are rumours that Trump wants to tear up (or 'reform') the World Trade Organization (WTO).[2] Real or not, the rumours signal that Uncle Sam is unhappy with the current international model.

This book documents how the US periodically alters the so-called trade and investment landscape as circumstances dictate. After World War Two, and with no global competitors, US planners sought to create a manageable, low-tariff trade and investment system to work in its interests, namely the General Agreement on Tariffs and Trade (GATT). Within a few decades, bilateral trade and investment treaties were being tested on weak economies. By the 1990s, as the more profitable elements of the US economy shifted from banking and manufacturing to financing and hi-technology, US strategists persuaded the political class to effectively replace GATT with the World Trade Organization (WTO), with more focus on intellectual property, patent protection and so on. More recently, as economic powers attempt to follow an independent course in global affairs, the

US is seeking to rewrite the rules of global trade and investment once again by promoting bilateral 'free trade'.

These seismic global shifts are merely a reflection of what US power has done historically, since at least the end of World War Two – namely that when the existing system makes other nations appear powerful by boosting their share of global GDP, thereby threatening elite US interests (the 'globalization paradox'), US strategists rewrite the rules of global trade and investment in order to continue privileging US businesses.[3]

But, be it 'liberal' global integration or 'conservative' nationalistic bilateralism, working people lose out. For example, Mexico signed on to NAFTA in the early 1990s and US jobs relocated there. In addition to these US factory closures, however, Mexican farmers failed to compete with US agribusiness. To give another example, when China joined the WTO in 2001, more US workers saw their factories move to China; but Mexican workers lost out to the Chinese competition, too.[4] Today, software and automation are putting jobs at risk in China, Mexico, the US and across the world, whether that software and automation are used by corporations stationed abroad or by those in US-based tax havens.[5]

The solution is offered neither by an adherence to a neat global order like TPP nor by Trump's brand of fanatical nationalism. Nor is it offered by the choice between a neoliberal European Union or an ultra-neoliberal Brexit. A US-UK 'free trade' deal will bring all of the worst elements of the (apparently) now-dead Transatlantic Trade and Investment Partnership to British workers and consumers, but without the mild protections of a political union. There needs to be a third way beyond 'liberal' internationalism and 'conservative' nationalism that puts human needs first and brings an end to the relentless privatization of our planet.

Part I

Reshaping globalization

1 Free trade: From World War Two to the World Trade Organization

How the US created an international trading system after the Second World War that would serve its leaders' political and economic interests. And how neoliberal policies came to be woven into the fabric of trading blocs.

Prior to the end of World War Two, British and American diplomats sought to create what became the United Nations. Through the UN, Britain and the US hoped to set international standards for conflict, trade and investment which they expected others to follow without necessarily following the rules themselves. With the War still raging, the US-led United Nations convened its Monetary and Financial Conference (Bretton Woods). There, it was agreed that the UN would establish the International Bank for Reconstruction and Development (World Bank) and the International Monetary Fund (IMF). The IMF is responsible for ensuring that international debtors make payments to their creditors.[1]

Until 1971, when gold-backed currency was deregulated, global financial markets were not particularly volatile. Bretton Woods imposed a global order of regulated capital, gold-backed currency and fixed exchange rates. A US Federal Reserve report says: 'Preparations for a new world trading order began during World War Two and date from the Atlantic Charter (August 1941) and the Lend-Lease (February 1942) agreements between the United States and the United Kingdom'.[2]

How did Russia and China react to this 'new world trading order'? The Soviet response to Bretton Woods was mixed.

Russia had been largely destroyed by Nazi Germany in the War and hoped to secure US reconstruction money. In exchange for Russia's participation in the Conference, the US agreed to credit the Soviet Union. But the Soviets were cautious about disclosing the weight of their gold deposits and refused to accept IMF jurisdiction over the rouble's exchange rate. The Soviets also wanted an extension on the upper limit of credit with the IMF, allowing them to borrow more to supplement official reserves before penalties could be imposed.

At the time of Bretton Woods, China was still fighting a civil war (1927-50). This was fought between the Kuomintang government of the Republic of China (now Taiwan), led by Chiang Kai-shek, and the Communist Party of China, led by Mao Zedong. Chiang's government was invited to Bretton Woods. The US hoped that Chiang would win the civil war and absorb China into the US-led global system. The fact that Mao won and led decades of nationalist statism is called 'the loss of China' by US ideologues.[3]

How did Britain with its post-War Labour government react to the new international order? Historian Raymond Vernon writes that the US-British establishment 'emphasized reconstruction as a necessary condition for the creation of a functioning global economy, requiring among other things the consolidation of the protectionist European states in a more efficient economic unit'. Ultimately, this was to lead to the formation of the European Union. The failed International Trade Organization (ITO) was 'more ambitious than any economic agreement negotiated up to that time, covering rules with respect to labor standards, economic development and international investment, foreign trade practices, restrictive business practices and inter-governmental commodity agreements'. Vernon goes on to note that 'the bulk of the ITO charter was the product of a relatively small group of technocrats from a very few countries, notably the United States, Great Britain and Canada'.[4]

The Executive Committee of the US Council of the International Chamber of Commerce said that the Charter of the ITO was 'dangerous... because it accepts practically all of the policies of economic nationalism'. Undermining the nationalism and nationalization of others has been a core goal of the US foreign-policy establishment, particularly since the end of World War Two. One of the ways in which the US dealt with the threat of 'dangerous... economic nationalism' was by drafting Friendship, Commerce and Navigation (FCN) treaties (later known as Bilateral Investment Treaties – BITs) with developing countries.[5]

The ITO charter also 'accept[ed] the principles of economic insulation', says the Federal Reserve report. The ITO largely failed, apparently because the US could not circumvent the demands of other members. It was replaced *de facto* by the General Agreement on Tariffs and Trade (GATT), which made bilateral negotiations easier. GATT also 'did not require Congressional approval'.[6]

At the UN Conference on Trade and Employment, the US, France, Britain and Canada founded GATT, which came into force at the onset of 1949. In the previous years, the US had worked hard behind the scenes to reduce global tariffs on trade in the hope of boosting its exports. In 1943, the British Labour MP and head of the British Board of Trade, Hugh Dalton, explained that a likely outcome of the GATT would be 'a series of bilateral arrangements between the US and the various Dominions, in which each of the latter would make concessions which would be helpful to them but not to us'.[7] Britain wanted to retain as much of its Empire as possible, but also understood that in order to be a significant player in the post-War world, it had to play second fiddle to the United States. More than this, however, we learn from Dalton that GATT and other multilateral bodies did include strong bilateral elements.

Dalton articulated the general concern that Britain was losing its international near-monopoly over trade and finance. Dean Acheson, head of the US Executive Committee on Economic Foreign Policy, explained in 1944 that: 'The pre-war network of trade barriers and trade discrimination, if allowed to come back into operation after this war, would greatly restrict the opportunities to revive and expand international trade.' US President Franklin D Roosevelt's Secretary of State, Cordell Hull, explained that America's aim was to impose 'a worldwide program of multilateral reduction in barriers to international trade... It is of fundamental importance to the interests of the

United States and to the establishment of the kind of economic conditions which we hope to see prevail in the post-war world.'[8]

After World War Two, 23 countries (each of them GATT members) accounted for 80 per cent of world trade. 'Under the "reciprocal mutual advantage" principle, no country would be forced to make any unilateral concessions', says the US Federal Reserve report. Tariffs were reduced for about half of the products comprising world trade and were 'concentrated on sectors that lacked the political strength to absolve them from consideration'. When a US corporation opened a business in a third-party country, it faced minimal tariffs on reimports. This amounted to a huge protection mechanism for US business: cheaper labour abroad (eg for assembly) and close-to-zero tariffs on reimported products.[9]

GATT as 'Globocop'

According to the US Federal Reserve report, it is 'difficult to attribute much of a role to the GATT in the dramatic economic recovery during the immediate post-war period beyond that of an effective supporting actor'. The 'actor' stagnated in the 1950s, particularly with regard to stimulating full employment. Where GATT was effective, however, was in threatening economic nationalism. By the time of GATT's stagnation, European policymakers were formulating an organization for post-War reconstruction, the intergovernmental Organization for European Economic Co-operation. France and Germany also signed bilateral investment – as opposed to trade – deals with 'Third World' (ie non-Western and non-Soviet) countries. Through GATT, the US established bilateral negotiations with European nations.[10]

By the third GATT session in August 1949, 133 bilateral negotiations had been completed by 34 countries. Like TPP and TTIP today, the arrangements were made in secret. '[The] tariff schedules were not expected to be made public until late in 1949', according to reports from the period. The arrangements were 'similar to the International Monetary Fund articles of agreement', said the ITO in 1949. The industrialized countries reduced tariffs on industrial products by around 36 per cent after the first five GATT rounds (between 1942 and 1962). According to World Trade Organization statistics, tariffs were reduced: by an average of 37 per cent in the Kennedy Round (1964-67); 33 per cent in the Tokyo Round (1973-79); and 38 per cent in the Uruguay Round (1986-94) which brought GATT to its end.[11]

The US reduced its tariffs by about 35 per cent, which 'was important for Western Europe because greater access to the US market enabled the countries to earn scarce dollar reserves, which could then be used to purchase US capital goods' (goods used for production not consumption). Multilateralism laid the trading foundations throughout the 1950s, 'although it became the method to eliminate tariffs within the European Economic Community'. Economist Karin Koch notes how 'growing protection in the United States' was a core reason why GATT stalled after the Kennedy Round; another was the refusal of Britain and the US to allow the graduated tariff reduction called for by other countries.[12] This was an early indication that the 'free trade' advocated by those countries was a myth.

What about GATT's effect on poorer countries? International trade specialist Kenneth J Vandevelde writes that GATT focused on trade, not investment. 'The GATT contained no provisions on investment, but it shifted the primary legal framework for international trade relations from bilateral to multilateral agreements and set in motion successive rounds of negotiations aimed at worldwide trade liberalization.' After World War Two, Latin American states imposed high tariffs, subsidized their industries and adopted several exchange rates. 'Often, import substitution industrialization was identified with socialism' in the minds of US planners, 'sometimes with an ethnic identity', like African or Arab 'socialism'.[13] Socialism was often a code word for economic independence, which corporations vehemently oppose. The 1950s saw a series of nationalizations in the Middle East and North Africa: Mossadeq's nationalization of Iran's oil; Qasim's nationalization of Iraqi oil; and Nasser's nationalization of Egypt's Suez Canal, a vital trading route for oil and other goods. In the early 1960s, Syria nationalized its foreign assets. 'By the 1980s, half of the mineral production in developing countries was state-owned.'[4]

Friendship, Commerce and Navigation (FCN) treaties drafted by the US were signed with third parties outside the GATT framework. They 'included the most elaborate provisions on investment ever seen'. They also included articles to grant US companies Most-favoured Nation (MFN) status (in effect, reducing tariffs for them) and access to courts of arbitration in case of trade and investment disputes. The post-War FCN treaties attempted to prevent the kind of 'socialism' (in other words, sovereign development) seen in Africa, Latin America and the Middle East (many of whose countries were members of the Non-Aligned Movement, founded in 1961 as a bloc that sided neither with the Soviet Union nor with the US).[15]

In 2004, Andrew K Rose conducted what he describes as 'the first comprehensive econometric study of the effect of the post-war multilateral agreements on trade', in which he pays particular attention to GATT. Though his work has been challenged, Rose maintains that 'membership in the GATT/WTO is *not* associated with enhanced trade, once standard factors have been taken into account' (the emphasis is in the original). Rose writes of 'the multilateral trade system as a GloboCop for all countries, independent of membership'.[16]

The GATT 'GloboCop' set the international standard even for countries that were not members. This prefigures Hillary Clinton's recent description of TPP as a 'gold standard' for international investment arrangements.

The dangers of bilateral investment treaties

Legal specialist Wayne Sachs noted that Bilateral Investment Treaties (BITs) 'are "new" in name only'. Sachs's article was one of the first legal papers to discuss BITs in the era of Trump's hero, Ronald Reagan. Unlike Free Trade Agreements (FTAs), BITs 'deal exclusively with matters related to investment'. The aim of a BIT is to 'ensure US investors unimpeded access to [the partner] economy on terms at least as favorable as those available to local and third-state investors'. Despite provisos about labour and environmental standards, as well as protections for 'democracy' in general, Sachs points out that US investors are given 'protection against non-commercial losses, whether caused by civil disorder or by government actions such as expropriation, nationalization, and confiscatory taxes and regulations'.[17]

So much for 'free' trade. In countries with significant national resources, nationalization can stimulate impressive socio-economic recovery, as seen for a brief period in oil-rich Venezuela and Brazil, until internal corruption and external influence destroyed the social project. In the absence of nationalization, health and living standards are polarized between those who can afford private services and those who cannot.[18]

Returning to Sachs' summary of BITs, he writes that they are a shield against taxation. Allowing US companies to go tax-free, or as good as tax-free, is another way of privatizing public services, running huge deficits and cutting back on social spending ('structural adjustment' in neoliberal parlance).[19]

Sachs notes that 'the government intends to use the BIT program to *create* international law'. So, in terms of creating international standards that even non-members are forced to follow ('Globocop') it does not matter whether they are multilateral agreements (like Clinton's TPP 'gold standard') or the bilateral deals that Trump prefers. 'Yet,' Sachs continues, 'the BITs also *rely* upon international law as a substantive standard' (the emphases are in the original). Such laws include provisions to allow corporations to sue governments.[20]

The US State Department's website lists three broad aims of Bilateral Investment Treaties. They are designed to: 'protect investment abroad... encourage the adoption of market-oriented domestic policies that treat private investment in an open, transparent, and non-discriminatory way; and support the development of international law standards consistent with these objectives'.[21]

On the first point: BITs are only nationalistic in the sense that they benefit national corporations. They undermine domestic workers and investors by allowing country x to open businesses or acquire businesses in country y. 'Nationalism' in this context really means US corporate dominance over other countries.

On point two: the 'encourage[ment]' of 'market-oriented' domestic policies is anathema to democracy. Take Britain's

National Health Service. Though there is overwhelming support for keeping it publicly owned, US tech firms and packaged medicine companies could include in BITs or FTAs provisions to privatize elements of the NHS.

The third point refers to the extent to which international law is US-led. The US frequently violates GATT and WTO treaties, but when other countries allegedly do so, it screams blue murder. The US seeks to wield enough influence over foreign governments to make sure they don't allow their corporations to compete too much with US businesses. In GATT and the WTO, there are provisions to allow a given country Most-Favoured Nation (MFN) status, though this is often difficult to attain. BITs are therefore an easier way to achieve 'most-favoured' status, allowing investors to be treated advantageously in a foreign country.

For instance, if the US wants to sell cars to a major car-producing country like Germany or South Korea, a BIT with those countries will include articles ensuring that they will not impose regulations (eg for health and safety or the environment) that they would not impose on their own domestic companies. The US State Department website explains that a BIT 'generally affords the better of national treatment or most-favored-nation treatment for the full life cycle of investment'.[22] In another scenario, if US financial institutions open branches in the UK, for example, an MFN clause in a US-UK BIT will prevent the British government from regulating that institution. This is problematic for the tax-paying public, because deregulation (which is part of the neoliberal project) inevitably tends to lead to financial collapse. It is also antithetical to democracy because it means that wealthy foreign interests not only access domestic markets (thus undermining local business), but they are not subject to extra taxes or regulations.

The US State Department website goes on to explain that BITs guard against expropriation as host nations are obliged to compensate US companies for alleged hindrances to profit. 'Performance requirements' are also included, meaning that if US companies perform badly in host countries they will not face penalties. 'BITs give investors from both Parties the right to submit an investment dispute with the treaty partner's government to international arbitration. There is no requirement to use that country's domestic courts'.[23]

BITs also allow US corporations to choose their managers, which further undermines domestic labour in the sense that qualified indigenous managers are not guaranteed employment in US companies operating in their country.

Bilateralism and human rights

In the 1980s, the Reagan administration signed BITs with several countries, most of them extremely poor. Early test-subjects included: Bangladesh (1986), Cameroon (1986), the Democratic Republic of Congo (DRC, 1984), the Republic of Congo (1990), Egypt (1986), Grenada (1986), Haiti (1983), Senegal (1983) and Turkey (1985). Let's look at the DRC, also known for a time as Zaire.

In June 1960, the Belgian Congo became independent of its European master. Patrice Lumumba came to power on a popular vote and made clear his intentions to use Congo's resources in the interests of the Congolese: 'The exploitation of the mineral riches of the Congo should be primarily for the profit of our own people and other Africans', he told New York businesspeople. In September 1960, President Kasa-Vubu dismissed Lumumba, who was prime minister for under three months before the British, Belgian and US intelligence services conspired to murder him.[24]

MI6 officer and later British peer, Daphne Park, was asked if MI6 was involved in Lumumba's assassination. 'I organized it', said Park. The BBC acknowledges: 'Lumumba made a fateful step – he turned to the Soviet Union for help [economic and military]. This set off panic in London and Washington.' Lumumba and his supporters, Maurice Mpolo and Joseph Okita, were tortured and executed by forces from Belgium and Congo's Katanga region, before being dissolved in acid.[25]

From the South African Truth and Reconciliation Commission we learn that British intelligence plotted Operation Celeste, the murder of UN Secretary-General Dag Hammarskjöld, who died in a plane crash. Hammarskjöld refused to withdraw UN troops from Congo, fearing further massacres between the warring factions. MI5 and the Special Operations Executive were involved in the plot, which was hatched in apartheid South Africa via the South African Institute for Maritime Research. The CIA was also involved. Letters exchanged between agencies state: 'Dag is becoming troublesome... and should be removed... I want his removal to be handled more efficiently than was Patrice.' The plan was to explode Hammarskjöld's plane with a bomb allegedly supplied by Union Minière, a Belgian mining company with private interests in the copper-rich Katanga region.[26]

In 1965, Lumumba's pro-US Chief of Staff for the Congolese National Army, Mobutu Sese Seko, came to power. Mobuto quickly garnered an international reputation for brutality, banning political parties and crushing secessionist movements. By 1984, when the US signed its first ever BIT with the country, Congo was importing 60 per cent of its food, despite having plenty of arable land; half of all Congolese children died before the age of five; and wages were 10 per cent of what they had been prior to independence. The *New York Times* reported at the time: 'Zaire has one of Africa's largest markets and a liberal investment code.'[27]

The BIT stated that the objective was 'to provide US investors with significant investment guarantees and assurances as a way of inducing additional foreign investment'. Another aim was 'to encourage, and facilitate participation by private enterprise to the maximum extent practicable'. It also noted: 'Each of these models was developed after lengthy and extensive consultations within the US Government and with the private sector.'[28]

As well as the generic misery and mass deaths that come with propping up a dictator, one of the other anti-democratic facets of the treaty is the fact that US companies could now sue the Congo government for alleged inhibitions to profits. Later in the book, we discuss investor-State dispute settlements (ISDS) and how they undermine governments; in the meantime, the following brief example describes the concept. In 1993, the firm American Manufacturing Trading sued Zaire in an ISDS case 'based on the provisions of a [BIT]'. The lawsuit chides Mobutu's failure to prevent looting of foreign-owned corporations. It says that this is the fault of the Congolese people (technically 'the government'), who must compensate the US company.[29]

Neoliberalism enshrined: the Maastricht Treaty

The modern European Union (EU) was from its outset a neoliberal project, achieved via the Maastricht Treaty of 1992 and the Lisbon Treaty of 2009, and complete with its own currency (the euro) as of 1999.

In macroeconomic terms, public-sector debt can be a necessity. After World War Two, for instance, Britain's public-sector debt reached levels above that of the First World War, but within five years the debt had declined to pre-War levels. By the 1970s, public-sector debt was lower than at any time since the late 1880s. One reason for the impressive book-balancing was a vast social spending programme by the Labour government: on reconstruction, the welfare state and the National Health Service.[30]

But under Maastricht rules, new members of the EU were obliged to cut social provision under the pretext of keeping debts and deficits in check – even in times of harsh recession. 'The freer internal market tends to increase the disparities between regions within [European Community] countries', wrote Michael Clarke of the Royal Institute of International Affairs in the early 1990s. 'In a relative sense, the rich will get richer and the poor will get poorer after 1992' – as indeed they did.[31]

Political scientists Robert Bohrer and Alex Tan note that Maastricht 'brought austerity across the member states, in spite of high levels of unemployment in the region'. It mattered not that 13 out of 15 governments were in fact leftwing. European Monetary Union (EMU) countries were committed to keeping their deficits under three per cent of GDP and their national debts at less than 60 per cent. By the end of 1997, 14 out of the 15 countries had met the target, 'due to austerity measures and more flexible economic conditions'. The pattern was repeated more severely after the financial crisis that began in 2008, when European Union member states imposed crushing austerity on their populations while meeting private-sector debt repayment which, under complex purchasing agreements (like gilts), are held in the public sector.[32]

Returning to the late 1990s, having proved that they could punish their populations sufficiently with austerity, 11 countries were admitted to the European Monetary Union. These measures were particularly cruel in light of the recession hitting Europe at the time. Germany's unemployment, for instance, was then worse than at any time since the 1930s. Bohrer and Tan speak of 'austerity *required* by the Maastricht criteria' [emphasis added], with governments 'unable (or unwilling) to stem the tide of unemployment by expensive propositions such as expanding the public sector'.[33] They note the European Union's 'general retrenchment of welfare state benefits... as countries seek to remain in the acceptable deficit and debt zones', before adding: 'Europe, like other regions, has witnessed an erosion of domestic control over economics as a result of global competition'. They warn that 'the heady days of nationalization and heavy state intervention' were over.[34]

NAFTA: 'a stunning setback'

As Europe entered a disastrous single currency and neoliberal period, in 1993 the US, Canada and Mexico entered into a trilateral agreement: the North American Free Trade Agreement (NAFTA).

Former US Trade Representative Carla A Hills writes that NAFTA 'prohibited barriers such as local-content and import-substitution rules, which require producers to ensure that specified inputs are produced domestically'.[35] Consequently, domestic production in Canada and especially Mexico was harmed. Two million Mexican farmers went out of business thanks to cheap and subsidized US agricultural imports. Many tried to enter the US in search of work and were met with President Clinton's wall, Operation Gatekeeper.

According to the US Chamber of Commerce, six million jobs currently depend on US-Mexico trade and a further eight million on US-Canada trade. Thanks to NAFTA, Canada exports 98 per cent of its oil to the US. Under NAFTA, Mexico took on the role of an assembly plant for US products. '[A] large percentage of that output returns home [ie to the US] as imports of intermediate goods, which allows US firms to focus on the higher-end task of assembling finished products.'[35] Sandra Polaski, at the time Deputy Undersecretary for International Affairs at the United States Department of Labor, says that by the time NAFTA was imposed, arrangements were 'concentrated in the auto parts, electronics, and apparel sectors' and that Mexico was transformed into a service provider, with its large labour force assembling goods for re-export to the US, much like China today.[36]

What about the human costs of NAFTA for the United States and especially Mexico?

Mexico's ex-Finance Minister, Jorge G Castañeda, notes that in Mexico, 'aggregate incomes have not risen much, in real terms, since NAFTA entered into force'. As with the effect of the Maastricht Treaty in Europe, NAFTA in North America stopped Mexico 'from returning to the old days of protectionism and large-scale nationalizations and caused the prices of tradable goods on both sides of the border to converge'. Large-scale privatizations followed Mexico's economic structural-adjustment programmes imposed by the IMF in the 1980s. Prior to that, Mexico had enjoyed a period of comparative prosperity. Economist Vincent Dropsy notes that before 1970, Mexico imposed a 'stabilizing development' policy, based on import substitution (in other words, self-sufficiency), high growth and low inflation.[37]

Under Maastricht, the policies of leftwing and rightwing European governments blended because supranational policy came to dictate fiscal and monetary outcomes. The same applied to Mexico after NAFTA. Castañeda writes: 'NAFTA did provide life support to what the writer Mario Vargas Llosa famously called "the perfect dictatorship", which otherwise might have succumbed to the democratic wave sweeping Latin America, eastern Europe, Africa, and Asia.' Castañeda concludes that real incomes have stagnated in Mexico across the entire economy.[38]

Undoing many of its 1970s poverty-reduction policies, Mexico initiated neoliberal economic reforms in the 1980s, laying the groundwork for further reductions and eliminations of tariffs.

Devaluation of the peso in 1994-95 crashed much of the Mexican economy, setting the US dollar against the already weaker peso. It resulted in a 'stunning setback in wages' (Polaski). Economist Andreas Waldkirch writes that limits on foreign direct investment in Mexico were removed as part of major law liberalizations in 1989. This facilitated further privatization and privileged US businesses. 'Most of the fluctuation in [Mexico's] services sector is due to large acquisitions in banking.' While the proportion of Mexico's agricultural jobs fell from 25.7 per cent to 17.3 per cent, under NAFTA, employment in its financial-services sector grew by 6 per cent.[39]

Waldkirch goes on to note that US firms operating abroad tend to do better than domestic businesses. This is due in part to a technological advantage: inventions subsidized by the taxpayer (often under the cover of military research and development) are given to private interests and used in foreign countries – including Mexico and the UK – by US corporations.[40]

Continuing with the human costs, the collapse of the peso gave the US Clinton administration the opportunity to lend the Mexican government – in other words, the Mexican taxpayer – $47 billion, not including interest. The loan drew on the Treasury Department's Exchange Stabilization Fund, bolstered by the IMF and the Bank for International Settlements. Clinton had previously failed to receive Congressional approval and moved to justify the bailout 'as a matter of "national security"' according to two analysts in the journal *Latin American Perspectives*. 'Since the devaluation [of the peso] made cheap Mexican labor even cheaper while weakening demand for US products, this turnaround affected the US job market.'[41] According to the US Labor Department, over 98,000 US jobs were lost in the first two years of NAFTA. The Mexican Confederation of National Chambers of Commerce meanwhile estimates that NAFTA 'had a negative impact on 60 per cent of commercial establishments in Mexico'.[42]

Mexico experienced an 11-per-cent wage decline in the manufacturing sector between 1994 and 2001, despite the fact that productivity grew by 50 per cent. People were putting in longer hours for less pay. The World Bank estimates that rural poverty in Mexico rose by three per cent in four years. Mexico's environmental-safety investments declined by 45 per cent in the first few years of NAFTA. Air pollution nearly doubled. Overall poverty increased by seven per cent between 1994 and 1998.[43]

But in 2001 when it joined the World Trade Organization, an even cheaper, more oppressed labour force entered the arena: China's. This led to the closure of 500 *maquiladoras** between 2001 and 2002, with many US firms offshoring to Asia.[44]

In 2004, Sandra Polaski submitted a briefing note to the Canadian Standing Senate Committee on Foreign Affairs. According to her findings, 90 per cent of Mexicans' incomes fell or stabilized after NAFTA. Only 10 per cent profited. Today, 31 per cent of the Mexican population lives in abject poverty, slightly higher than the pre-NAFTA period. This statistic includes, however, the 1970s and early 1980s, when socialistic reforms led to poverty reduction. 'Mexico cut tariffs deeply and was exposed to competition from its giant neighbors', including even more impoverished and oppressed populations, such as Colombians. Polaski concludes: 'The experience of Mexico confirms the prediction of trade theory, that there will be winners and losers from trade. The losers may be as numerous as, or even more numerous than, the winners, especially in the short-to-medium term'; in other words, the timescale used by corporations in their quarterly profit measures.[45]

In late September 2018 the Trump administration concluded its 'renegotiation' of NAFTA, renaming it the US-Mexico-Canada Agreement The broad aims were to penetrate more Canadian markets and privilege US biotech companies.

World Trade Organization: 'significant differences'

Trade in services is managed via GATT's successor, the WTO. It is regulated by three pieces of legislation: the General Agreement on Trade in Services (GATS), its Annex on Financial Services and the Understanding on Commitments in Financial

---

* Maquiladoras are factories, often subcontracted by foreign corporations, which export raw materials and take advantage of cheap labour, often in poor countries. The products assembled in the maquiladoras are usually re-imported to the richer countries of origin for their consumer markets.

Services. Whereas the US's domestic Gramm-Leach-Bliley Act requires the Federal Reserve to monitor and regulate foreign financial institutions operating in the US, the GATS provision at the WTO (with some exceptions, to which I shall return) allows foreign banks (including US banks operating abroad) 'greater scope to compete in other countries on the same basis as domestic banks and under the same regulations'.[46]

The US pushed for further neoliberal policies along the lines of Maastricht and NAFTA multilaterally through the WTO. But rising powers China and India blocked US efforts by raising barriers to protect their own industries. The Congressional Research Service says that the WTO Doha Round (2001) was problematic because nine years of negotiations over numerous issues reached stalemate. They included domestic subsidy reduction and market penetration concerning agriculture, industry, intellectual property, non-tariff barriers and special/ differential treatment for poor countries. 'The most significant differences have been between developed countries, led by the United States and European Union, on the one hand, and developing countries, led by India, Brazil, and China, on the other hand.' The US was then diverted to its so-called war on terror from 2001 and the invasion of Iraq in 2003.[47]

India's behaviour at the WTO demonstrates at least two things: how WTO policy liberalizes national economies; and how, even with US bilateral trade and investment liberalization, some sovereign states can get 'too big for their boots'.

The US and EU 'were the most influential in setting WTO rules', write Shaffer et al, who argue that the WTO has affected the laws of Brazil, China and especially India at the state level, making those countries more open to trade, transparent to international investigations and reliant on state subsidies to stimulate private services. They refer to this as 'globalized localisms'. Prior to 1991, India was a largely closed economy. Ninety-four per cent of its tariff rules were unaffected by GATT. There was zero growth in per-capita income during the 1960s and 1970s, not least because of fast population growth, which 'left a significant percentage ... in extreme poverty'. The growth of the Asian Tigers and the oil shock of the Gulf War in 1991 forced India to confront its comparative isolation. India's political elites permitted the IMF to interfere in the economy and open it up to international trade.[48]

This culminated in India's adoption of the General Agreement on Trade in Services at the WTO. Under WTO rules, the US challenged India's trade-related aspects of intellectual property (TRIPS), restrictions on balance of payments and its industrial policy. As with the Mexico-NAFTA example, India's accession to the WTO increased its share of global trade – in this case from 0.66 per cent to 2.23 per cent by 2013. Growth was highly concentrated. As part of its Strategies and Preparedness for Trade and Globalisation agenda (2003-10), run by the United Nations Conference on Trade and Development (UNCTAD) and the UK's Department for International Development (DFID), India accepted outside 'advice' on how best to integrate into the WTO. In the UK, the British tax-funded initiative is sold to the public as 'aid to India'.[49]

By 2008, the WTO had one foot in the grave after the Doha Round (2001) stalled when the EU (mainly Britain) and the US disagreed with other countries' agricultural subsidies, which both parties considered to be market interference. The US offered to cap farm subsidies and increase work visas in exchange for more concessions from poor countries, especially Brazil, China and India. India was particularly concerned that elimination of its special safeguard mechanism (SSM), which protects domestic farmers, would put millions of farmers and consumers at risk of unemployment and starvation. In the UK, former Labour minister Peter Mandelson described the US Food, Conservation and Energy Act 2008 as 'one of the most reactionary farm bills in the history of the US'.[50] It amounted to protection for US agribusiness while the US attempted to dismantle protectionist mechanisms in other countries. Again, such is the reality of 'free trade'.

2 Free trade: The Bush and Obama years

How the US came to see the post-War trade and investment order as outdated and how they drafted new arrangements accordingly.

AFTER World War Two US-created multilateral bodies ushered in 'a new world trading order' (as the Federal Reserve called it). Working in the interests of big US businesses, these bodies included GATT, post-Maastricht Europe, the WTO and NAFTA. Weapons in the form of bilateral 'free trade' agreements and bilateral investment treaties were also available when individually tailored deals were needed.

After the collapse of the Soviet Union in the early 1990s, the US's enthusiasm for large trade and investment blocs like the European Union diminished. An article in the establishment publication *Foreign Affairs* (analysed in depth in this chapter) discussed the 'new global economic order' of the immediate post-Soviet era, as opposed to that of the post-World War Two period. Not much is really 'new', said the authors. US-based transnational corporations (TNCs) seek to undermine labour unions, environmental protections, state controls over national economies and opposition to their profit-making.[1]

What was new, however, was the growing use of bilateralism in negotiating 'free trade'. Referring to the post-Soviet era, the article noted that of apparent concern for US policymakers and their TNC constituents was the growth of Japan and Europe, both of which the US had facilitated after World War Two with the Marshall Plan (an example of the 'globalization paradox' mentioned in the Introduction). By 1992, intra-firm investment flows (such as Ford Europe to Ford USA) accounted for 40 per cent of all US 'trade', compared to foreign-investment flows, which accounted for only 10 per cent. Explaining what corporations mean by globalization, the authors noted that 'Growing numbers of firms rely on diverse partnerships around the world for know-how, components and selected product offerings in order to compete at home and abroad.' This can include global design networks and stock exchanges.[2]

The key point was that the US-led post-Soviet order was more concerned with 'access for investment' than with borders, as well as with 'fair market competition' – meaning in large part the elimination of state controls. We have already seen the effect that investment access had on Mexico's currency. The aim of these 'market access regime[s]' is to 'upset the structure of existing international economic agreements', the authors continued. 'Policymakers can no longer depend mainly on multilateral trade agreements.' This is exactly what Trump is now saying: that multilateral deals need to be renegotiated from the bottom up or dismantled and replaced with bilateral ones. By the 1980s, the US was losing out to Japanese automobiles and semiconductors. Through mergers, acquisitions and shared technologies (like the IBM-Siemens project) the US battled the competition. The article's authors cautioned that although Toshiba, Apple and IBM agreed to co-operate over research and development, Europe and Japan continued to subsidize and protect their own industries.[3]

The authors of the *Foreign Affairs* article stated:

The strategic problem for the United States is that, although its interests are global, many of the most pressing negotiations need to be bilateral or regional. The United States needs multilateralism to ensure that the playing field is level and to safeguard against becoming entangled in its own web of contradictory bilateral deals. At issue, then, is how to reconcile global arrangements with specialized agreements...

When issues get more complicated, problems of negotiation increase. Getting more than a hundred GATT members to agree on a comprehensive package covering a wide range of complicated trade issues simply overloaded the Uruguay Round negotiations... Governments should concentrate more on bilateral and minilateral efforts to manage the practical details and then multilateralize them from the bottom up.[4]

Free trade agreements

At the time of writing, the US has signed Free Trade Agreements (FTAs) with 20 countries. FTAs can be signed with one (bilateral) or more (multilateral) countries. They can include provisions on investment, but they mostly relate to trade and allow US companies access to foreign markets. FTAs are different from Bilateral Investment Treaties (BITs) which are specific to financial investments.

The US's first FTA was signed with Israel in 1985. The agreement sought to integrate Israel into the US-led world economic system. To quote the FTA, it focuses on the 'expansion of world trade' via the 'removal of trade barriers' in 'mutual interest'. The FTA with Israel was 'consistent' with GATT rules. After the agreement was signed, the US's loans – as opposed to 'aid' – to Israel ceased. By 1990, grants tripled. Burgeoning US military and tech firms opened up in Israel, particularly through the Binational Industrial Research and Development funds. US exports to the country more than doubled and imports quadrupled. Israeli investment in the US also increased, as did US investment in Israel.[5]

Historian Bernard Reich notes: 'The bulk of US military aid to Israel is used to purchase military items produced in the United States. This is a clear case in which foreign aid creates jobs in the donor country.' Reich goes on: 'Given the amount of aid that never leaves the United States, the total amount of US aid to Israel actually overstates its contribution to the Israeli economy.' Reich concludes that 'only a small percentage of US military grants is spent in Israel itself, and most of the economic grant aid is devoted to servicing loans used to finance past weapon sales'.[6]

Trade specialist Howard Rosen writes that the US-Israel FTA set a precedent for future US trade policy. One US objective was to counter the European Community-Israel bilateral deal signed in 1975. The US-Israel FTA 'was a convenient way for the United States to demonstrate that it would not wait for the rest of the world before moving ahead on trade liberalization'. This echoes Trump today. He is not going to wait for Japan to agree with the US over TPP provisions or for Europe to agree over TTIP. Rosen goes on to say that the 'growth in US exports to Israel seems to be concentrated in high-technology products'.[7]

The US did not sign another FTA until 1992.

Trump has criticized Democratic President Bill Clinton and his wife, Hillary, for their ratification/support of NAFTA. However, Trump neglected to mention that it was his own Republican Party under President George HW Bush (Bush I) that signed NAFTA into law in December 1992. Outgoing President Bush I signed two FTAs: one with Canada, the other with Mexico. Both FTAs introduced NAFTA and signalled 'our confidence in economic freedom', in the words of the President. Mexico had already proven itself with a 'bold reform program', boosting US 'trade' (which often means intra-company trade).[8]

By including Canada and Mexico on its list of FTAs and as part of NAFTA, the US State Department signalled that its perception of trade deals is both bilateral and multilateral. They are multilateral in that more than two nations have signed on (like the failed Trans-Pacific Partnership), but they are bilateral in that the US can withdraw from the multilateral treaty and maintain bilateral relations with one or more signatories. This is important because it means that the 'noodle bowl' of bilateralism can go ahead even in the absence of multilateralism.

In her book *Living History* (2003), then-Senator Hillary Clinton wrote that domestic 'healthcare... had to compete with other legislative priorities'. According to Clinton, Treasury Secretary Lloyd Bentsen, Secretary of State Warren Christopher and economic adviser Robert Rubin 'were adamant about postponing healthcare reform and moving forward with [NAFTA]'. Clinton claims that the cabinet 'believed' in NAFTA's potential to aid US 'economic recovery' and create 'the largest free trade zone in the world'. Clinton acknowledged that NAFTA was 'unpopular with labor unions' but said it was 'an important administration goal'.[9] This is one of many examples of the democratic deficit in the US.

Assault on Central America

Under George W Bush (Bush II), the US signed a NAFTA-type deal with the Central American states: CAFTA-DR (Central American-Dominican Republic Free Trade Agreement). It started as a series of bilateral FTA negotiations.

With the exception of Costa Rica, the US has intervened and/or supported military dictatorships in all of the CAFTA member states. Costa Rica has no significant military and relies on the United States. The IMF in 2000 called the 1980s 'a lost decade' for Costa Rica, El Salvador, Guatemala, Honduras and Nicaragua and went on to note: 'Contributing factors included the armed conflicts in El Salvador, Guatemala and Nicaragua (which also had adverse effects on the economies of Costa Rica and Honduras)'.[10] In most cases, the civil wars and use of death squads, often trained and armed by the US with British support, caused a long-term decline in socio-economic indicators.

'From the Second World War until 1972, Central American countries had remarkably stable currencies', according to a scholarly study of the region. 'A complementary explanation was the presence of repressive dictatorships in El Salvador, Guatemala and Nicaragua. In all three countries', the study continued, 'the incomes of the peasantry and urban poor people and workers did not keep up with per capita growth'. The situation became really dire in the 1970s, with most Central American economies experiencing a decline in wages and employment and a rise in overcrowding as peasant farmers fled from conflict areas to city slums.[11]

Let's look at some examples.

El Salvador. In the 1980s, the country was plagued by death squads – armed groups conducting extrajudicial killings or 'disappearances'. The death squads' activities were bent on crushing social progress which might lead to the kind of 'dangerous economic nationalism' feared by the post-war US planners. The overwhelming majority of aid, military equipment and training for the death squads was provided by the US. Britain also played a role. In November 1977, a 'decision was made' by the UK government 'to sell armoured

Privatized Planet

vehicles and other military equipment to the Government of
El Salvador'. In 1985, it was revealed in Parliament that Britain
'offered places for one or two suitably qualified Salvadorean
[sic] officers to attend Staff college courses [at military
academies] in Britain'.[12]

In 1987, Islington North MP (and future leader of the British
Labour Party) Jeremy Corbyn revealed: 'In addition to offering
bilateral aid to the El Salvadorean Government, the British
Government are also undertaking the training of one El
Salvadorean officer at the British military academy'.[13]

Guatemala. Between 1982 and 1983 alone, President Ríos
Montt slaughtered 1,771 indigenous Maya people. Britain's
military base in the region is in neighbouring Belize. A British
intelligence report from the period stated: 'There has been a
certain amount of official involvement in murder and political
violence. "Death Squads" have been part of the Guatemalan
way of life for many years.' Despite acknowledging this
appalling human rights environment, Britain's Prime Minister
Margaret Thatcher dispatched British troops stationed in Belize
to Guatemala to assist Ríos Montt in his war against peasant
land reformers.[14]

British paratrooper Gus Hales recalls: 'We were a bit trigger-
happy and pumped up, and looking for something to come
up.' The commander of the British Forces in Belize, Brigadier
Pollard, held secret meetings with Guatemalan military
officers, including Colonel Tobar Martínez, who had allegedly
massacred 251 villagers in Las Dos Erres. At the base in Belize,
a British police officer, Alan Jenks, ran the special branch,
which placed alleged guerrilla suspects under surveillance.[15]

Nicaragua. The leftwing Sandinistas overthrew the
US-backed Somoza dictatorship in 1979. Counter-revolutionary
(*Contra*) forces, backed by the US, committed shocking war
crimes in the fighting that followed. US policy on the small
country was condemned by the World Court in 1986, despite
efforts by Britain and Japan to block the Court's ruling.
Nicaragua's brief transition from dictatorship to subsistence
and wealth redistribution was described by Oxfam in 1989 as
The Threat of a Good Example?[16]

Honduras. In the 1970s and 1980s, the US-trained and armed

Battalion 316 'carried out a campaign of torture, extrajudicial killing, and state-sponsored terror against Honduran civilians', according to the Center for Justice and Accountability. Honduras was also a 'staging ground' for covert US wars in Guatemala and Nicaragua.[17]

Although the outgoing Democratic President Bill Clinton signed the US-Jordan Free Trade Agreement in 2000, the Bush II years (2001-09) saw the emergence of most US bilateral FTAs. A year before signing up to CAFTA, the US signed bilateral FTAs with its would-be members, just as it had signed bilateral FTAs with Mexico and Canada before the multilateral NAFTA: in 2004 Costa Rica, Dominican Republic, El Salvador, Guatemala, Honduras and Nicaragua all signed FTAs with the US.

The CAFTA legislation reads much the same as the NAFTA text. Along with the usual vague provisos about protecting workers' rights and the environment, CAFTA seeks to '[enhance] the competitiveness of [signatories'] firms in global markets', with the aim of 'establishing *the Free Trade Area of the Americas*' (the italics are in the original). Local markets had been largely impaired, if not devastated, in the preceding war years. CAFTA allows US corporations to take their wealth, power, government subsidies and expertise to poor countries and use the labour of those poor countries. It also demands that US firms be treated as if they were national companies, meaning that taxes, duties, tariffs and fines are reduced. This is called 'national treatment'. 'Each Party shall accord national treatment to the goods of another Party.'[18]

Central America is rich in gas, oil, coal, fruits, beans, plants, livestock, metals and precious stones. It also has a large population of impoverished, exploitable workers. CAFTA includes provisions for US companies to extract natural resources from the signatories. Chapter 3 includes articles for vehicle and travel liberalization, making it easier and quicker to transport and export extracted resources duty-free.[19]

The global textiles, clothing, leather and footwear industries, particularly in Central and South America, have been negatively affected by two major occurrences. The first was the dismantling of the international Multifibre Arrangement in 2005, which removed limits and quotas for goods and services related to this industry. The second was the financial crisis of 2008, which wiped out 11 million full-time jobs and 3 million part-time jobs, many of them in Latin America. Profits went up 9.9 per cent between 2005 and 2011.[20]

Many Central Americans rely on local textile manufacturing for their livelihoods, including 'hand-loomed fabrics of a cottage industry' and 'traditional folklore handicraft goods'. CAFTA technically includes protection for such industries. However, the inclusion of investor-State dispute settlement clauses means that powerful corporations could threaten to or actually sue governments for passing domestic legislation to protect independent textile and garment workers. In addition, it excludes protection if it affects Most-Favoured Nation preferences.[21]

Stemming the 'pink tide'

Shortly after CAFTA was signed, a devastating turn of events (for the US) transpired: a number of leftwing governments came to power in the 2000s and 2010s in Latin America. They included those led by Daniel Ortega of Nicaragua, Manuel Zelaya of Honduras, Álvaro Colom of Guatemala, Mauricio Funes of El Salvador, Leonel Fernández of the Dominican Republic and Luis Guillermo Solís of Costa Rica.

US analysts do not consider these governments to be as radical as 'communists' ('Reds'), hence they describe them as 'pink'. The drift towards progressive left-centrism has been nicknamed the 'pink tide' by US commentators. Like European governments after Maastricht, 'most members of the [pink] tide have worked to address social-welfare concerns within the general confines of market mechanisms', says Latin America specialist Craig Arceneaux. He also writes that 'although exasperation over neoliberalism spurred the political change, free markets are hardly endangered in Latin America'. Interestingly, the pro-free market Frazer Institute gave Latin America 5.3 out of 10 for neoliberalism in 1990, when much of the violence was raging; 6.5 in 2000, during recovery; and 6.6 in 2008.[22]

Chapter 1 of this book noted how Europe's neoliberal reforms in the 1980s, and especially post-Maastricht in the 1990s, undermined democracy by shifting left-leaning governments further to the right. Latin America expert Katherine Isbester documents a similar pattern in her specialist region. 'The weak state lacks autonomy from the elite class but the elite no longer control the vote' – hence the weakening of status quo politics. 'Most Pink Tide countries have compromised with the neoliberal structuring of their political economy and the insertion of their nations into globalization.' Isbester also writes that NAFTA, CAFTA and the WTO have the effect of 'locking in neoliberalism, [so] the room for deep reform to the organization of the economy is limited'.[23]

Recent events in Honduras indicate a return to the not-so-distant past. In Honduras, President Zelaya undermined CAFTA by guaranteeing a minimum wage, working more closely with the Bolivarian Alternative for the Americas (ALBA) bloc and calling for a national Constituent Assembly. In 2008, Zelaya attempted to extend his presidency by backing a new ballot. A Honduran Supreme Court order found Zelaya guilty of violating an injunction issued against him over the ballot. He was overthrown in a US-backed military coup in 2009. Regional specialists José Briceño-Ruiz and Isidro Morales write that the coup 'did away with the relationship between Honduras and the Bolivarian axis'. The new leader, Porfirio Lobo, 'intensified and accelerated efforts to conclude the negotiations of a free trade agreement with Canada', which has also signed a multilateral FTA with the EU: the Comprehensive Economic and Trade Agreement.[24]

In her 2014 book, *Hard Choices*, Hillary Clinton expresses her fear that democracy could take hold in Latin America by belittling Honduras, 'home to about eight million of the poorest people in Latin America. Its history has been marked by a seemingly endless parade of discord and disasters'.[25] Clinton omits the US role. She describes Zelaya as 'a throwback to the caricature of Central American strongman, with his white cowboy hat, dark black moustache, and fondness for Hugo Chávez and Fidel Castro'. Clinton feared the US looking 'isolated in our own backyard'.

Interestingly, the following passage in which Clinton admits

US involvement in the post-coup period was removed from the paperback edition of *Hard Choices*:

> We strategized on a plan to restore order in Honduras and ensure that free and fair elections could be held quickly and legitimately, which would render the question of Zelaya moot and give the Honduran people a chance to choose their own future [and] began looking for a respected elder statesman who could act as a mediator.

Clinton chose Óscar Arias of Costa Rica. Arias is 'respected' because he follows US orders, unlike the allegedly pro-Chávez Zelaya. Compared with the rest of the region's nations, Costa Rica 'has one of the highest per-capita incomes and greenest economies in Central America'. Clinton neglects to mention that it's also the regional country least subject to US invasions and proxy wars.

By the end of January 2017, at least 123 Honduran environmental and land activists had been murdered by gangs, police and the military. The Civic Council of Popular and Indigenous Organizations of Honduras (COPINH) is an organization comprised of 200 ethnic Lenca communities. COPINH was led by Berta Cáceres, one of the country's leading environmentalists. Cáceres organized against the Agua Zarca dam. The dam, funded by European companies (Voith Hydro and Siemens), risks desiccating the Gualcarque river and harming farming communities. In 2013, soldiers close to the Honduran company overseeing the dam opened fire on peaceful demonstrators, killing indigenous leader Tomás García. Cáceres was murdered in her home in 2016.[26]

Trump may be tough on refugees and immigrants, but Obama was not far behind.

The *New York Times*, not known for its radical leftism, ran a story headlined 'Obama's Death Sentence for Young Refugees', referring to the closed-border policy which most mainstream news ignored until Trump cranked it up a notch. The paper reported that President Obama and Mexican President Peña Nieto had agreed to intercept Central American refugees trying to reach the US via Mexico. Reporter Nicholas Kristof wrote: 'In effect, we have pressured and bribed Mexico to do our dirty work, detaining and deporting people fleeing gangs in Honduras, El Salvador and Guatemala.' Kristof concluded: 'The American-Mexican collusion began in 2014 after a surge of Central Americans crossed into the US, including 50,000 unaccompanied children.'[27]

This coincided with the end of the Pink Tide and the re-emergence of the old death-squad and drug-gang politics in many countries. When journalist Juan Gonzáles quizzed Hillary Clinton about her involvement in the coup and future plans for Honduras, she replied:

> I think we need to do more of a Colombian plan for Central America, because remember what was going on in Colombia when first my husband and then followed by President Bush had Plan Colombia, which was to try to use our leverage to rein in the government in their actions against the [Revolutionary Armed Forces of Colombia (FARC)] and the guerrillas, but also to help the government stop the advance of the FARC and guerrillas, and now we're in the middle of peace talks. It didn't happen overnight; it took a number of years. But I want to see a much more comprehensive approach toward Central America, because it's not just Honduras.[28]

This is an astonishing statement, given what Plan Colombia actually involved, namely stepping up US military aid. 'Peace talks' came after years of intensified counter-revolutionary violence against civilians, three-quarters of which was the responsibility of state forces and their related gangs.

For decades, Colombian elites used the military and paramilitaries to crush land reformers, student unions, environmentalists and the leftist FARC. Since the 1980s, British special forces, along with US forces, have armed and trained the Colombian military, which in turn trains the paramilitaries. In 2001, the British Parliament revealed the true scope of Plan Colombia and its human rights consequences: 'The United States in its push for a military solution will waive Plan Colombia's human rights preconditions for military aid to the army for the second time when the plan is reviewed... effectively sanctioning more massacres, displacements, assassinations, torture and disappearances of the unarmed population'.[29]

Other South American countries – Argentina, Brazil and Chile – are also experiencing a shift to the Right and a predictable surge in US investment.

The Trans-Pacific Partnership

The Trans-Pacific Partnership began life in secret in 2006 – under the Republican Bush II administration – as a series of negotiations and talks between corporate lawyers and politicians in the US. (Most people think it started in 2009, but the Center for Responsive Politics cites much earlier lobbying documents.) This gigantic multilateral FTA was led by the US and included 11 would-be signatories: Australia, Brunei, Canada, Chile, Japan, Malaysia, Mexico, New Zealand, Peru, Singapore and Vietnam. The talks excluded China. TPP would cover 40 per cent of global trade and create a market for 800 million consumers.

Trump is praised by some working-class Americans for wanting to rip up trade and investment deals and replace them with 'free and fair trade', in his words, and with products bearing those 'beautiful words', Made in America. But Trump's speechwriters could be sued for plagiarism. In 2015, President Obama's speechwriters said exactly the same thing in justifying Obama's signing into law the Trans-Pacific Partnership (TPP): 'So we can export more products stamped Made in America all over the world that support higher-paying American jobs here at home,' said Obama. 'Over the summer [of 2015], Democrats and Republicans in Congress came together to help the United States negotiate agreements for free and fair trade that would support our workers, our businesses, and our economy as a whole.'[30]

How did environmentalists respond to the text? Despite assurances that TPP gives the 'strongest' environmental protections of any trade agreement to date, over 450 environmental groups, including Bold Alliance, Environmental Network, Friends of the Earth, the Sierra Club and SustainUS, signed an oppositional letter to Congress. Jane Kleeb of Bold

Alliance said: 'The TPP will create a scenario for landowners where they are at the mercy of big oil and big gas to do whatever they want with our land and water, using secret courts and backroom deals.'[31]

What about labour and trade unions? According to its website, the American Federation of Labor-Congress of Industrial Organizations (AFL-CIO) 'organized to fight against [TPP]'. The union's position was strong: 'The final TPP will not create jobs, protect the environment or ensure safe imports. Rather, it appears modeled after [NAFTA]'. It described NAFTA as 'a free trade agreement that boosts global corporate profits while leaving working families behind'. In conclusion, it stated: 'The grim conditions facing workers in TPP partner countries were not effectively addressed in the TPP text or the side agreements called "consistency plans".' For AFL-CIO, 'too many commitments to improve labor rights and environmental practices are vague, and the proposed enforcement scheme relies wholly on the discretion of the next administration'.[32]

The Center for Responsive Politics lists, in descending order of mentions in letters to Congress, the following companies as key TPP lobbyists (not complete here): Nike, the US Chamber of Commerce, the Business Roundtable, Ford Motors, Pfizer, the National Pork Producers Council, AFL-CIO, the Nucor Group, Merck & Co., Outdoor Industry Association, Buhler Quality Yarns, Glen Raven Mills, National Spinning, the Association of Global Automakers, Philip Morris, Google, Time Warner, Novartis AG, the National Cotton Council, Walmart, Visa, Boeing, General Motors, Monsanto (now part of Bayer), ExxonMobil, JPMorgan Chase, American Apparel and Footwear, Bank of America and Pepsi.[33]

This list suggests that US companies wanted US Asian labour to continue making clothes for European and American consumers, as well as to open up new drug markets for the emerging 'middle class' that can afford them.

Obama gave a talk to TPP-sponsor Nike in Oregon, explaining the alleged benefits of TPP for big and small businesses. (Nike in general has a terrible record on human rights in its factories based in poor countries.) The US relied on TPP-esque deals, said Obama, because 'if we don't write the rules for trade around the world – guess what – China will. And they'll write those rules in a way that gives Chinese workers and Chinese businesses the upper hand, and locks American-made goods out'. Trump's rhetoric is big on bringing jobs (and profits) back to the US but, as Obama points out, 'outsourcing is already giving way to insourcing. Companies are starting to move back here to do more advanced manufacturing, and this is a trend we expect to continue'.[34]

According to CNN, between January 2010 and June 2013, Obama's Secretary of State, Hillary Clinton, made 45 pro-TPP statements in talks, speeches and interviews to foreign ministers, thinktanks and other organizations.[35] In *Hard Choices*, Clinton says that TPP will enable the US to 'engag[e]' Vietnam. More importantly, however, it will 'link markets throughout Asia and the Americas, lowering trade barriers while raising standards on labor, the environment, and intellectual property'. She provides no evidence for the claim. Clinton quotes Obama: TPP will give 'American companies' access to Asia because they 'have often been locked out of those markets'. Clinton says TPP will be 'important for American workers, who [will] benefit from competing on a more level playing field'. Evidence: none.

Getting closer to reality, Clinton writes that TPP will 'strengthen the position of the [US] in Asia'. She acknowledges that 'globalization and the expansion of international trade brings costs as well as benefits'. The pros and cons are not identified or discussed. 'TPP won't be perfect', she says, 'but its higher standards, if implemented and enforced, should benefit American business and workers'. Evidence: none. TPP will 'cover a third of world trade'.[36]

The Transatlantic Trade and Investment Partnership

The Transatlantic Trade and Investment Partnership (TTIP) started life in 2011, when several US and European organizations published a letter. The authors represented: the US Chamber of Commerce, BusinessEurope, the US Council of International Business and others. The letter was sent to Europe's Commissioner for Trade, Karel De Gucht, and to the US Deputy Assistant to the President (and future Trade Representative), Michael Froman. It concerned 'the reinvigoration' of a US-EU Investment Dialogue. The corporate collective set in motion a series of policies that would guarantee investor rights across all manner of European services and industries.[37]

One of the organizations' goals was to develop 'a co-ordinated approach' to dealing with third parties, including 'addressing competitive distortions that may arise with state-owned enterprises'. Anything owned by taxpayers is a market distortion to private interests. The businesses adhere to 'the fundamental principle that investors and their investments should be treated equally under the law regardless of nationality'. US corporations operating in the UK, France, Germany, throughout the EU, want the same rights as European corporations. Generally speaking, this ideal applies to corporate persons, not to actual persons, such as workers who cannot get visas, or refugees and migrants who are often sent back home to face torture or death.[38]

The letter says that, in order to maintain this 'principle of non-discrimination', it is necessary to establish 'predictability in government administration', meaning that socialist policies, such as those promoted by popular movements (Corbynism in the UK, Sandersism in the US, Podemos in Spain, and so on), must be rendered ineffective by domestic legislation which would prevent popular parties and governments implementing pro-social reforms.[39]

In the letter, the Chambers of Commerce say that bilateral harmonization treaties should include clauses for 'avoiding any semblance of arbitrary and capricious action by government officials'. For Trump, these kinds of assurance are easier to work out on a one-to-one basis than through multilateral deals like TTIP. What should concern activists, however, is the fact that much of the TPP and TTIP texts are simply cut and pasted into bilateral FTAs and BITs.

In 2012, policymakers discussed the broad objectives of the letter and began arranging the biggest regulatory merger in history. The talks were held in secret and developed further at the G8 summit, from which Russia was soon expelled. On 17

June 2013, the following representatives met at the Lough Erne Resort in Northern Ireland, to announce TTIP: US President Obama; British Prime Minister David Cameron; European Commission President José Manuel Barroso; and European Council President Herman Van Rompuy.

Barroso spoke about deregulation (or 'reducing red tape') and about 'avoiding divergent regulations for the future'. Barroso cited 'the business communities on both sides of the Atlantic' and bragged of their 'strong advoca[cy] of free trade and investment'.[40] The report by the Confederation of British Industry (CBI) on TTIP suggested the deal's potential to 'open up public procurement contracts to the highest degree possible' – in other words, privatize all remaining public services.[41] Another CBI report laid down its demands: government should start 'increasing our aviation capacity; scrapping the immigration cap' so that skilled and semi-skilled workers can drive down wage inflation; 'improving access to trade finance', meaning deregulation; 'and keeping the UK in a reformed EU, which is outward-looking, signing free trade agreements with high-growth markets, starting with TTIP'.[42]

3 Free trade: The Trump years

Why President Trump really pulled out of multilateral trade deals – and why the new agenda suits some big US businesses even better.

President Trump is portrayed as a dangerous idiot. But what does President Trump really know or care about 'free trade'?

In his book, *The America We Deserve* (2000), Trump wrote: 'We need tougher negotiations, not protectionist walls around America. We need to ensure that foreign markets in Japan and France and Germany and Saudi Arabia are as open to our products as our country is to theirs.' Trump complained that 'America has been ripped off by virtually every country we do business with'. His attitude to trade is thus: 'It's become a cliché to say that business, especially trade, is like war… But, cliché or not, it's true.'[1]

In *Time to Get Tough* (2011, updated in 2016), Trump wrote of his desire to 'make America money by brokering big deals'. 'The President's duty', says Trump, is not to execute the wishes of Congress on behalf of voters, but rather: 'to create an environment where free and fair markets can flourish, private-sector jobs can be created, and our economy can boom'. On international free trade agreements (FTAs), Trump wrote of 'the embarrassing and anemic deals Obama has pulled off… I'm for free and fair trade. After all, I do business all over the world'. A particularly bad agreement, as far as Trump is concerned, is the US-South Korea FTA, signed under Obama. 'It was so bad, so embarrassing, that you can hardly believe anyone would sign such a thing'. Trump's complaint was that it gave too much to the South Koreans at the expense of the US.[2]

Trump is driven by making a profit: 'America's business

is business', he continued. 'A president... [can] create an environment that allows the rest of us – entrepreneurs, small businessmen, big businessmen – to make America rich.' He went on to say that 'money is *itself* a weapon' (emphasis in the original).

In *Great Again* (2016), Trump wrote: 'We need legislation that gives American companies the tax priorities and financial support to create more of their technology.' This refers to giant tax cuts. Trump, by implication, wants to bring US wages, health and safety and environmental regulation down to the level of Mexico. He writes: 'A German auto company was all set to build a plant in Tennessee, but then it changed its mind and is building it in Mexico instead... the American labor force is the best there is', he concluded. 'We just have to allow them to compete.'[3]

Turning the tide on TPP

Even before it was published in October 2015, big business was unhappy with the final Trans-Pacific Partnership (TPP) draft because it failed to include measures to protect maximal US profits. The Trump administration, implementing the wishes of automakers, steel producers and other big US corporations, pulled out of TPP and stalled on TTIP. They did so for several reasons. It is important to understand them in order to anticipate what might come next if TPP and TTIP are renegotiated or replaced with bilateral deals, such as a US-UK 'free trade' deal.[4] Some US big businesses were unhappy that TPP excluded provisions to protect them from:

- *Currency manipulation.* Countries can weaken the value of their currencies in order to boost exports. US businesses consider this cheating because consumers might buy foreign products instead of US ones. To the chagrin of large US businesses, there was nothing in TPP to address this.
- *Value-added taxes.* When a US product is sold in a foreign country, those foreign governments slap a tax on the US product (VAT). This hurts US corporate profit, so the corporations wanted it dealt with in the TPP, but it was not.
- *Tax-inversions.* US corporations lose money by paying domestic taxes, so they merge with foreign companies and

enjoy tax holidays by moving abroad. But then US business has to follow foreign rules. They were hoping that TPP would rectify this by allowing them to follow US rules abroad.

- *Offshoring.* US businesses move abroad to take advantage of cheap labour. But as the US becomes a hi-tech-based economy, many businesses, like IBM, no longer need to go abroad because they can use software instead of humans. Elements of TPP made it easier to offshore, but technology changes made offshoring less relevant to some companies.

As the World Trade Organization's negotiations on trade in services and intellectual property stalled because the emerging powers demanded more concessions from the rich world, the US found itself increasingly challenged over alleged violations of WTO rules. The US was even challenged by its neighbour, Mexico.

A scholarly study of NAFTA and the WTO finds that 'Mexico won in several trade dispute cases with the United States'. Mexico challenged the US's protectionist measures on tuna and bovine labelling. This led to challenges by Mexico through the WTO over tomatoes and shrimps. Mexico emerged triumphant.[5]

India challenged the US, in particular over its imposition of countervailing duties on imports of certain hot rolled carbon steel flat products. Under GATT rules, included in the WTO, India claimed that the US's protectionist measures contravened the US Tariff Act on customs duties. Also citing GATT, India complained that the US violates its non-immigrant temporary working visas agreement. China, America's main competitor, also challenged the US at the WTO, which China joined later than India, in 2001. Citing the US Department of Commerce's claim that majority government ownership makes a given enterprise a public body, China claimed that the US was unfairly subsidizing its domestic industries. In the same complaint, China alleged that the US was levying import duties on Chinese products including solar panels, steel sinks and drill pipes.[6]

In addition, the US challenged these and other states at the WTO. For people like Trump, the optimal deal is a bilateral one in which any alleged misconduct on the part of the co-signatory can be met with swift US retribution at a US-based court of arbitration, as we saw in the Congo mining case.

So, why choose bilateralism over multilateralism? Trade specialist Young Jong Choi writes that a 'region-wide FTA is more profitable than subregional or bilateral FTAs'. However, Chris Dent of the Evian Group points out that 'in bilateral FTAs, the stronger partner' – in other words, the US – 'can have the power to influence the terms of FTAs more in its own favour'. Pascal Lamy, formerly Director General of the WTO, described bilateral deals as 'an instrument to get "brownie points" and gain an advantage over other WTO Members'.[7]

The belief that Trump and Trump alone smashed Obama's multilateral model is, however, unfounded. Much earlier, in 1994, the Clinton administration had laid the groundwork when it published a Bilateral Investment Treaty (BIT) prototype, which was signed by several countries, many of which were ex-Soviet states. The standard Preamble mentions workers' and environmental rights, but also makes clear that these obligations are non-binding. Among its goals are: 'economic co-operation on investment issues; the stimulation of economic development; higher living standards; promotion of respect for internationally recognized worker rights; and maintenance of health, safety, and environmental measures. While the Preamble does not impose binding obligations, its statement of goals may assist in interpreting the Treaty.' Note that 'rights' are non-binding in BITs.[8]

The environment fares no better. Having agreed to the possibility of being sued by the US for alleged hindrance to profit-making, the co-signatory also agrees to Article 12(3), which states that 'each Party retains the right to exercise discretion with respect to regulatory, compliance, investigatory, and prosecutorial matters, and to make decisions regarding the allocation of resources to enforcement with respect to other environmental matters.'[9]

In 2012, during the Obama presidency, the State Department led by Hillary Clinton published a new template for BITs. It shows that the US government's priority for trade and investment undermines the social and civil rights of the co-signatories and their businesses. The model treaty states 'that agreement on the treatment to be accorded such investment will stimulate the flow of private capital and the economic development of the Parties'. There are provisions to protect 'national law', but these are met with the line 'as well as through international arbitration'. It is worth noting that taxpayers have to pay for their governments to be sued by the US at international (usually US-based) courts of arbitration. This makes governments less likely to challenge US businesses.[10]

Trump and bilateral deals

Trump has made it clear that bilateral trade agreements, like those with Congo and Honduras outlined in the previous chapters, are more beneficial to US corporations than multilateral ones like NAFTA, TPP and TTIP.

But why is this so? It is not just the US that uses bilateral FTAs. London School of Economics specialist Dr Stephen Woolcock writes that the European Union recently 'shifted to a trade policy that envisages a greater use of [FTAs]'. The big one was supposed to be the multilateral TTIP. However, Woolcock notes 'greater emphasis on bilateral FTAs within its commitment to multilateralism in trade'. As far as the EU is concerned, 'region-to-region agreements have been difficult and slow to negotiate, in no small measure because the EU's partner region is often unable to make much progress towards integration'. If this model is accurate, it is easy to understand why maximal profit values in TPP were difficult to achieve. Woolcock says that certain EU states were 'motivated by a desire to achieve in FTAs what [they had] failed to achieve in multilateral negotiations'. This, he says, includes market access and trade-investment rules (so-called Singapore issues), 'trade facilitation, transparency in government procurement, investment and competition... in one form or another in FTAs'.[11]

In short, bilateral agreements are a way of speeding up neoliberal globalization, but of a kind less familiar to the public than NAFTA, TPP, or any of the multilateral agreements. In conclusion, Woolcock notes that failure in the WTO's Doha

Round (2001) to advance neoliberal reforms, a shift in US policy towards multilateralism (until recently at least), the growth of the Asian economies and a moratorium on FTAs by the EU's Trade Commissioner, Pascal Lamy, caused the EU to shift its policy.[12]

Bilateral agreements create what Demet Yilmazkuday and Hakan Yilmazkuday call an 'asymmetry', where the stronger of the given partners dictates the rules. The lack of enforcement mechanisms in multilateral agreements 'creates a structural problem of rules in trade agreements that will self-enforce the trading countries to achieve more liberal trade'. The authors also note that 'transportation costs, differences in country sizes and comparative advantages are all obstacles for having a multilateral FTA'.[13]

Studies cited by the authors indicate that 'when countries are asymmetric in terms of endowments, global free trade is stable (for a large set of parameters) only through bilateral agreements'. As the US has excluded its only economic competitor, China, from multilateral deals like TPP, it makes sense for the US to negotiate bilateral ones.

Baier and Bergstrand (cited by the Yilmazkudays) note the following preferences for bilateralism over multilateralism:

(i) the closer in distance are two trading partners; (ii) the more remote a natural pair is from the rest of the world (ROW); (iii) the larger and more similar economically (in terms of real gross domestic products (GDPs)) are two trading partners; (iv) the greater the difference in comparative advantages; and (v) the less is the difference in comparative advantages of the member countries relative to that of the ROW [rest of the world].[14]

Although Trump plans to trade and invest bilaterally, the results will be the same if not worse for US workers than for the rest of the world: privatization, tax cuts for the wealthy, a race to the bottom for international and domestic labour and weakened environment protection. Bilateral agreements also aim to crush domestic research and development via intellectual property rules.

Trump's commitment to 'free trade'

As soon as Trump was sworn in as President, he instructed his Trade Representative, Michael Froman, to begin formal withdrawal from TPP. On 23 January 2017, Trump signed a memo directing Froman 'to withdraw the United States as a signatory to the Trans-Pacific Partnership (TPP), to permanently withdraw the United States from TPP negotiations, and to begin pursuing, wherever possible, bilateral trade negotiations to promote American industry'. Trump then called or met with several heads of state from the TPP countries to push for bilateral deals.[15]

Consider the following examples of Trump's bilateral business and military talk with foreign heads of state. They indicate the direction in which trade and militarism are going.

Trump and Canadian Prime Minister Justin Trudeau issued a joint statement. In addition to the usual provisos about keeping up environmental and labour standards, it read: 'We will continue our dialogue on regulatory issues and pursue shared regulatory outcomes that are business-friendly, reduce costs, and increase economic efficiency.' The joint statement also notes: 'US-Canada energy and environmental co-operation are inextricably linked, and we commit to further improving our ties in those areas. We have built the world's largest energy trading relationship.' This includes the Keystone XL pipeline, to which both parties are 'committed'. As for arms expansion, the US thanked Canada for considering 'the immediate acquisition of 18 new Super Hornet aircraft as an interim capability to supplement the CF-18s until the permanent replacement is ready'.[16]

Trump and Japan's Prime Minister Shinzo Abe also issued a joint statement: 'The United States and Japan reaffirmed the importance of both deepening their trade and investment relations and of their continued efforts in promoting trade, economic growth, and high standards throughout the Asia-Pacific region.' Interestingly, the joint statement reveals that the team behind Trump considered TPP as too unfriendly to business. It wasn't 'free trade' enough. The statement continues: 'Toward this end, and noting that the United States has withdrawn from the Trans-Pacific Partnership, the leaders pledged to explore how best to accomplish these shared objectives'. It notes that 'this will include discussions between the United States and Japan on a bilateral framework as well as Japan continuing to advance regional progress on the basis of existing initiatives'.[17]

Trump and New Zealand Prime Minister Bill English spoke on the phone. According to the White House: 'The two leaders affirmed the close friendship and bilateral partnership... [They] discussed regional issues, including challenges to regional peace and security.' That can be translated as: they discussed ways to counter China's growing regional influence. Trump 'affirmed' to English 'the US commitment to strong and active engagement in Asia', meaning the build-up of navy forces, including aircraft carriers. Indeed, Trump announced his intention to expand the Navy to include 12 aircraft carriers early in his Presidency.[18]

Trump told Peru's President Pedro Pablo Kuczynski: 'Peru has been a fantastic neighbor. We've had great relationships – better now than ever before... we're going to talk some business. I understand they're going to be buying quite a bit of our military – some of our military vehicles.'[19]

Australia wanted to keep the 'best' aspects of TPP. Australia's Trade Minister Steven Ciobo said: 'There were a lot of hard-fought gains that were achieved through intense negotiations over many years, in relation to the TPP. I don't want, and I know a number of other countries don't want to let those gains slip through our fingers... That's why I put a focus on whether or not we could have, for example, a TPP 12 minus one', meaning without the US. 'We'll be having a meeting in Chile in March of this year [2017] to canvass all of the options.'[20]

The above tells us that the worst aspects of TPP will be kept by Trump but the structure is being changed. Trump is now working one-to-one to undermine democracy, environmental regulations and public ownership, instead of through big trade blocs.

4 Rivalries: 'Globalization is a brutal process'

How the 'national interest' plays out in trade deals, from Canada to China, from India to Russia.

Western countries have, as previous chapters have shown, pursued their national interests by attempting to forge a global trade and investment structure. This is regularly called the 'rules-based order' by Western politicians. Often this involves propping up dictatorships (the oil-rich Saudis, for example), investing in countries with authoritarian regimes (China), sanctioning non-compliant governments (Iran), draining countries' resources (the minerals of Papua New Guinea) and of course supporting political coups (Brazil).[1]

Declassified documents from the post-World War Two era alone prove that this has been British policy for decades. In the 1950s, for example, when Kenyan nationalism was threatening Britain's murderous grip on the country, former Prime Minister Winston Churchill explained to the British-born landholder and former Kenyan Minister of Agriculture, Michael Blundell, that the Mau Mau rebels and their supporters were worse than mere savages: 'They're savages armed with ideas – much more difficult to deal with' than savages indoctrinated to obey authority, such as those brainwashed into subservience by, for instance, Christian missionaries. Continuing the theme of disrupting nationalism, in 1960 Britain's Joint Intelligence Committee explained: 'If... the Cuban revolution succeeds in achieving a stable regime which appears to meet the aspirations of the depressed classes, there will be a serious risk that it will inspire similar revolutions elsewhere in Latin America'.[2]

Historian Johan Galtung compares Soviet ambitions with

those of the US and concludes that the objective, imperialism, was the same, but with the values inverted. At the fifth Congress of the Polish United Workers' Party in 1968, Soviet President Brezhnev explained that 'when internal and external forces that are hostile to Socialism try to turn the development of some socialist country towards the restoration of a capitalist regime... it becomes... a common problem and concern of all Socialist countries.'[3]

The wretched Soviet dictatorship imposed by Lenin and Stalin and continued by successive governments until its collapse in 1991 was called 'socialism' and 'communism' by its rulers in order to try to give it a veneer of legitimacy. In reality, it meant state monopoly over planning, production and economics to the benefit of corrupt elites, just as 'capitalism' (or more accurately neoliberalism) really means institutionalized greed, state subsidies and exploitation for profit. Brezhnev continued: 'military assistance... is an extraordinary step, dictated by necessity.'[4]

In other words, those in power, be they 'communist' or 'capitalist', want to stop other countries from developing independent of their influence.

Even today the same kind of attitude is easy to find in establishment circles. A report by the Royal Institute for International Affairs (Chatham House), for example, cautions that: 'The risks to international order are real... Rising economic power has reawakened sovereign claims.' In other words, countries are pursuing their own national interests, not those of the Western powers. It recommends that regional deals, including the Trans-Pacific Partnership and Transatlantic Trade and Investment Partnership, 'should remain open to other countries willing to sign up to their rules'. The report notes that the Asian economies (particularly China and India) are re-linking GDP to population density, meaning that the largest populations on earth, China and India, have the potential to overtake the US and Europe in terms of economic power.[5]

It goes on to say: 'Globalization is a brutal process. Societies accustomed to being at the top of the pyramid are being forced to make harsh structural adjustments' in order to keep their GDPs high; hence the austerity policies of the past decade which have killed literally thousands of people. The report concludes: 'It will be important... to engage rising powers inside existing international institutions as equal partners' – though this may be interpreted as the illusion of equality. 'Some institutions and agreements', namely the Nuclear Non-Proliferation Treaty and the UN Security Council, 'are probably unreformable, given the vested interests of their privileged members. But others, such as the International Energy Agency, the World Bank and the IMF, can be reformed, with the G20 often playing an enabling role.'[6]

Documents like these reflect the attitudes of international policy planners. Let us look at some examples of states following their 'national interests' and working on trade and investment structures that are apparently beyond US control.

Canada's deal with the European Union: CETA

Between 2009 and 2014, the political elite of the European Commission in Brussels negotiated with the elite in Canada to broker an EU-Canadian trade and (mostly) investment deal, the Comprehensive Economic and Trade Agreement (CETA). The CETA text, made public in 2014, is mostly a cut and paste of Articles from NAFTA and related treaties. It concerns the dismantling of state-owned enterprises, the elimination of so-called non-tariff barriers to trade and the standardization of international regulations.[7]

In 2014, Cam Vidler, Director of International Policy at the Canadian Chamber of Commerce, delivered a talk about CETA. Vidler explained that the Chamber represents 20,000 businesses, big and small. The speech revealed that informal discussions began in 2007 between the Chamber and its European counterparts. Notice the total lack of input from unions, environmental groups and governments, as well as the lack of media coverage. Once governments were involved, the Chambers set the framework for discussion, Vidler continues.

The core of CETA is the inclusion of investor-State dispute settlement clauses. These help to ensure that governments, which might potentially be formed of the representatives of social movements, do not have too much power over corporations and wealthy investors. Vidler concludes: 'CETA resolved a great number of bilateral trade barriers, the EU reserved certain issues, particularly in the area of regulatory co-operation, for their negotiations with the US.'[8]

How did the US react? It would seem that the US under Obama actually favoured CETA because its success or failure was a litmus test for TTIP or other FTAs and BITs that the US might want to pursue. As US ambassador Anthony Gardner explained to Chatham House in the dying days of the Obama administration: 'We hope that the EU-Canada agreement is signed soon as this would be an important indicator that the EU is capable of concluding FTAs despite the trend against free trade in the EU.' Gardner's comments on bilateralism versus multilateralism not only prove that the origins of the two-pronged assault predate Trump, but are worth quoting at length in order to understand the US position on balancing bilateralism and multilateralism. First, Gardner quotes the German Marshall Fund-European Centre for International Political Economy (his ellipses): 'Theological debates about the relative merits of "multilateralism versus bilateralism" must... be placed in the context of what has happened in the real world'.[9] He goes on:

> As emerging economies have assumed greater importance in the global trading system and as non-tariff barriers have become more important than tariff barriers as obstacles to trade liberalization, it has been difficult to get consensus within the WTO. Significant external pressure is needed to invigorate the multilateral process.[10]

Finally, he quotes the Peterson Institute for International Economics: 'A successful effort to resolve disagreements across the Atlantic could become a template for the stalled global trade talks in several difficult areas, from agriculture to cross-border rules on services, investment and regulations.'[11]

Because NAFTA was a deal between the elites of the United States, Canada and Mexico, Britain was excluded from it. However, the UK government has stated that it has used its relationship with the US to gain access to Mexico via NAFTA. It is possible that the US will do the same in Europe via its close relationship with Canada.[12]

China: the new Silk Road

The media image of China as a rising dragon about to swallow up the world with yellow currency is a xenophobic myth. In the real world, once the nationalistic Mao Zedong (whose secret offers of a US-Chinese collaborative partnership were rejected by Washington) was out of the picture, the US moved into China economically, encouraging it to borrow billions of dollars from the US-led World Bank and International Monetary Fund. China's GDP ballooned, as did its national debts. Although the government retained control over industry, US foreign direct investments poured in and markets, especially housing, were financialized.[13]

The only real 'threat' that China poses to the US is that it might pursue an independent course in global affairs – hence the massive US military build-up in the Asia-Pacific region (the 'pivot to Asia' as the Obama administration called it.[14]

According to a report from 2009 by the business-linked US Council on Foreign Relations, China has pursued a nationalistic agenda since the 1990s, challenging NATO and Japan, both key US tools of influence and, in the case of Japan, with considerable regional influence. China's alleged move towards independence is mixed, however; it has 'enhanc[ed] its position with other major powers in the region, particularly Japan and the United States'. The Trans-Pacific Partnership was designed in part to create a regional framework to which China would have to adhere. The US report notes: 'Coping with China in a multilateral setting not only gives' smaller, regional nations (such as Vietnam and Singapore) 'the power of collective bargaining but also enhances their security'.[15]

In 1991, a newly reformed China joined the Asia-Pacific Economic Cooperation (APEC) grouping. APEC was promoted in the late 1980s by Australia's neoliberal champion, Prime Minister Bob Hawke. The US joined the APEC 21, as did Russia, and describes it as 'the premier forum for facilitating economic growth, co-operation, trade and investment'.[16]

Founded in the 1960s, the Association of Southeast Asian Nations (ASEAN) contrasts with APEC in that it initially excluded the United States. It has grown as a regional, mutual-interest bloc which has succeeded in making the region a nuclear weapons-free zone – minus Japan, which probably hosts US nuclear missiles, and China, which developed nuclear weapons in the 1960s. China is not a member of ASEAN, but has associate status through various treaties, one of which is the ASEAN-China Free Trade Area signed in 2002.[17]

In 2001, China, Kazakhstan, Kyrgyzstan, Russia and Tajikistan formed the Shanghai Cooperation Organization (SCO). In 2017, both India and its supposed enemy, Pakistan, joined SCO. The project is designed to integrate countries in the region, co-operate on military affairs and expand infrastructure projects.[18]

In 2006, the APEC states entered into negotiating the Free Trade Area of the Asia-Pacific (FTAAP), which since 2010 has been the third-largest economic bloc in the world.[19]

At the ASEAN Summit in Cambodia in 2012, a couple of years after achieving this status, several countries entered into negotiations for a Regional Comprehensive Economic Partnership (RCEP), a kind of TPP, but in favour of China (supposedly). The agreement created one of the biggest economies in the world ($49.5 trillion) and included 3.4 billion people. Both FTAAP and the ASEAN-China FTA seem to have stalled with the advent of RCEP.[20]

In 2013, President Xi Jinping announced China's new Silk Road Economic Belt in a speech delivered in Kazakhstan. The supposed aim (again recalling the real meaning of 'national interest') is to foster economic, trade and cultural co-operation across Eurasia and Southeast Asia. This is a rival to the US's Silk Road Strategy Act 1999, which sought to absorb some of the ex-Soviet states into the 'free market'. In 2011, having occupied Afghanistan (a key route along the 'Silk Road') for a decade, Obama announced a New Silk Road of America to capture South Asia's 'population of more than 1.6 billion people', as well as its 'vast energy resources – including oil, gas, and hydropower'.[21]

India: signing up to the global market

In addition to participating in some of the above trade and investment agreements, India's economy has been largely Americanized since its adoption of 'free market' principles in the 1990s.

After India dismissed the British, the rulers maintained a relatively closed economy until the early 1990s. Unlike the brutal Maoist model in neighbouring China, which had mixed effects, ranging from genocidal levels of starvation to improved infant mortality and life expectancy, India's poverty-induced death toll failed to bring about improvements in living conditions for hundreds of millions of people. With rivals like China gaining power and enemies like Pakistan gaining prestige, India decided to boost its GDP and join the 'free market'. This included turning large parts of the country into sweatshops, call centres and assembly plants for American and European businesses. This was called 'Shining India'. It also meant turning more of the agricultural sector into an export market, despite the fact that hunger and starvation affects a quarter of the population.[22]

According to a report by the rightwing Brookings Institution, despite joining the WTO, India has not strengthened its rules on intellectual property. This means that it retains some controls over domestic technology patents and drugs. This kind of protectionism has dissuaded the US from investing as much in India as it does, for example, in South Korea.[23]

Despite some political tensions, such as a border dispute, trade between India and China boomed from under $3 billion in 2000 to $66.57 billion by 2012. In 2017, however, India boycotted a meeting of 30 heads of state who discussed participation in China's Silk Road initiative. The so-called China-Pakistan corridor passes through Kashmir, a region whose status remains unresolved since the Partition of India in 1947 and the founding of Pakistan. India's opposition to the Silk Road might affect its relations with China at the Asian Infrastructure Investment Bank and the New Development Bank – both of which receive substantial British investments, to the chagrin of the US, which sees the banks as a threat to the World Bank.[24]

As for India's relationship with Russia, following the collapse of the Soviet Union, Kazakhstan suggested that the ex-Soviet states form a Eurasian Economic Union (EEU). It was not until 2015 that the EEU came into force. Its members are Armenia, Belarus, Kazakhstan, Kyrgyzstan and Russia. In 2017, India announced plans to work with Russia on a 'free trade' zone under the auspices of the EEU. *The Economic Times* (India) reports that such a deal could create a $37 billion or stronger market.[25]

Japan: doing a deal with Europe

During World War Two, the United States slaughtered three million Japanese people, many with incendiary bombs, burning to death over 80,000 civilians in a single bombing raid (9-10 March 1945). The new symbols of global power – atomic bombs – murdered a further 300,000 or so in Hiroshima and Nagasaki. Despite minor trade spats, like the protectionism of the 1980s imposed by Reagan in the US to guard American car corporations against superior Japanese vehicles, Japan has been largely subservient to US interests.[26]

Today, Japan hosts approximately 23 US military bases. After World War Two, the US made Japan include a peace clause in its Constitution. This was to ensure that the burgeoning US empire would not be challenged by a resurgent Japan. When it suited the US to use Japan as a proxy against a rising China, however, the Obama administration ordered Japan to revoke the peace clause in its Constitution, much to the opposition of the Japanese public. In 2006, Japan proposed forming a Comprehensive Economic Partnership for East Asia with Australia, China, India, New Zealand and South Korea but, at present, it has not been ratified.[27]

The subservience of Japan's political elite to the United States is so embarrassing that when Prime Minister Shinzo Abe (pronounced Abay) met Donald Trump in the US he actually uttered these words:

My name is Abe, but in the United States some people mistakenly pronounce my name as 'Abe'. But that is not bad, because even in Japan everybody knows the name of that great President, that a farmer and carpenter's son can become a President. And that fact, 150 years ago, surprised the Japanese, who were still under the shogunate rule. The Japanese opened their eyes to democracy. The United States is the champion of democracy.[28]

The US State Department refers to Abe as the kind of reformer it wants: easing monetary policy to tackle low growth; 'revisions to Japan's legal code; and pro-active Japanese government policies to welcome [foreign direct investment] and promote corporate restructuring'. The 'challenges' include Japan's 'insular and consensual business culture that is resistant to hostile mergers and acquisitions' and 'labor practices that tend to inhibit labor mobility'.[29]

Japan, meanwhile, has been engaging further with the European Union. There is a conspicuous lack of interest in the US, at least publicly, concerning the Japan-EU Free Trade Agreement (JEFTA). According to the European Commission's trade assessment impact, JEFTA is a response to TPP and is designed to boost trade between the EU and Japan, particularly in the timber, motor vehicle and services sectors.

Europe's trade assessment concludes that the main aim of JEFTA is to export more European-made products. One of the concerns, to give an example, is that Japan still retains some state controls over some of its services, despite Abe's reforms. This is particularly bothersome in the public railway services (PRS) sector, which is a significant mode of transportation for Japanese people and thus a hindrance to the European automobile producers. 'Ownership of PRS operators has been a critical topic of the EU-Japan FTA negotiations', says the trade assessment report. 'Concerns have been expressed about the possibility of more effective access to the sector given the former or current public ownership of PRS operators'. The report also envisages Japanese farmers requiring more skills in order to manage agriculture-related hi-technologies imported from Europe. The opening of 'large-scale production plants' might result in 'adjustments in labour' and the 'closure or sell-off' of smaller plants, the report concludes.[30]

Such casual euphemisms and abstract remarks about the loss of other people's jobs and incomes reflect the (lack of) commitment to democracy among Brussels' unelected elite. As the Chatham House report noted above says, globalization is a brutal process.

Russia walks an independent path

Following US-led efforts to facilitate the collapse of the Soviet Union, the ex-Soviet states and Russia adopted so-called neoliberal free markets (inevitably US-led) in the early 1990s. But when an ex-KGB agent, Vladimir Putin, came along and dismantled many 'free market' structures, US efforts to reinstate them began. A US military study looks back on the early Putin years and notes that, under Boris Yeltsin, Russia was 'economically depressed, militarily enfeebled, and dependent on Western assistance, giving the impression of being pliant and often subservient'. It goes on to lament that under Putin, there has been large-scale 'de-privatization'. The report notes that Russian nationalism and nationalization is an assault on 'Western values, such as respect for contracts and private property'. Putin's supposed nationalism is a 'major obstacle to a more constructive and legal international order'.[31]

Putin's moves provoked panic in Washington, as reflected in the New York elite media. An article in *Forbes* refers to Putin as the Shah of global oil and mourns that 'ExxonMobil is no longer the world's number-one oil producer... That title belongs to Putin Oil Corp – oh, whoops. I mean the title belongs to Rosneft, Russia's state-controlled oil company'.[32]

In 2011, Russia and the US fought a mini trade war over the former's accession to the WTO. The US Congress failed to adopt legislation granting Russia Most-Favoured Nation status. Russia retaliated by blocking GATT Article XIII, prohibiting imports. Shortly after the escalation of proxy wars between the three nuclear-armed powers (Russia versus Britain and the US), the US and the EU imposed sanctions. Obama signed executive orders sanctioning Russia. Ukraine is strategically significant because it is a key energy corridor, bringing Russian oil and gas to markets in Europe. In addition to the general policy of encircling Russia with missile systems in Turkey, Poland and

Romania, the US and EU negotiated 'free trade' deals with Ukraine during the reign of pro-Western leaders. The coup was, in part, an effort to make long-term investments in Ukraine safe for the US and European Union. In September 2014, the EU also tightened sanctions.[33]

With Trump in the White House and a former Exxon CEO, Rex Tillerson, briefly as Secretary of State, internal tensions over US policy on Russia were bound to escalate, with the establishment military and media keen to demonize Russia. Trump is allegedly eager to form business ties with Russia and Tillerson's Exxon is keen to keep its contracts. In 2017, Exxon sued the US government for a small fine ($2 million) the government had imposed over Exxon's three-year contract with Rosneft. During the contract, Exxon (then under Tillerson) showed 'reckless disregard' over the sanctions, according to the Treasury Department.[34]

Part II

Our environment

5 Activists: 'Get a life!'

Pollution kills millions of people around the world each year and carbon emissions continue to worsen the climate crisis. Yet Western policymakers are drafting 'free trade' legislation to make it even easier to produce, sell and use polluting products.

The Democratic administration of Barack Obama made very flawed efforts to penalize big polluters. As US Secretary of State Hillary Clinton travelled the world pushing fracking on ex-Soviet countries, she nevertheless pledged to move the US away from coal and onto green technologies. President Trump is now pushing both fracking *and* coalmining. While Clinton and Obama spied on climate agreements to try to weaken them (as we shall see), Trump is simply ripping them up.

Europe's triumphs and challenges

The European Union (EU) is rather like the US Democrats in this respect: weak on climate change, but better than nothing. Europe's so-called 2020 package is a set of laws supposedly designed to ensure that the EU matches its CO_2 emissions targets by that year. This involves a 20-per-cent cut in greenhouse-gas emissions, sourcing 20 per cent of EU energy from renewables and making a 20-per-cent improvement in energy efficiency. The pledges are facilitated under the EU's emissions trading scheme. A secret European Commission memorandum for Members of the European Parliament (MEPs) confirms that carbon price rises are too slow for industrial emissions reductions under the trading schemes. This gives industry a licence to pollute.[1]

Yet some countries are on track to meet their targets. During times of particularly high wind, Denmark has enough energy to meet not only its own domestic demands (which are high because of indoor heating needs), but also to share 80 per cent of its excess energy with Germany, Norway and Sweden. Norway is on target to meet half of its electricity needs by 2020. Over recent decades, Germany's use of renewable energy has tripled. By 2015, over a third of Germany's domestic energy needs were being met with renewables. The figure is expected to grow to 45 per cent by 2025. During peak wind-power periods, customers are paid to consume energy, which is great for consumers as Denmark and Germany have the highest electricity costs in Europe. Renewable sources generate 48 per cent of Portugal's electricity. In May 2016, Portugal survived for four days using only renewable energy. Between 2013 and 2016, the country added 550MW of wind capacity to its grid.[2]

These achievements might be overshadowed by the dark clouds of investment deregulation in the fossil-fuels sector, a move for which Trump and some European states are pushing. The President and CEO of the US Chamber of Commerce, Thomas J Donohue, says that 'while alternative and renewable energies are important, they cannot replace our more traditional sources of energy', meaning coal, gas and especially oil: 'Not now, and not in any of our lifetimes.' Donohue goes on to state: 'Fortunately, the United States has extraordinary reserves of untapped energy', which the shale gas 'revolution' (as the press dubs it) is unlocking. 'Europe has significant resources as well. And we have each other. We must work in concert to advance our collective energy security.' Now that Russian energy is impeded politically and to a degree physically from passing through Ukraine to Europe, Europe needs US energy. Donohue concludes that this arrangement 'makes perfect sense. America has it. Europe needs more of it. So let's build the necessary infrastructure so we can trade more energy'.[3]

Europe's second or third economic power (after Germany and France), the United Kingdom, is racing towards the climate-change cliff. In contrast to the achievements of Denmark, Germany and Portugal, the British government has pledged to 'halt the spread of onshore windfarms'. A Department of Energy and Climate Change spokesperson reiterated the government's 'commitment to end new onshore wind subsidies'. Former Environment Secretary and Conservative Member of Parliament Owen Paterson, says: 'There is no place for subsidising wind – a failed medieval technology which during the coldest day of the year so far produced only 0.75 per cent of the electricity load.' While disinvesting in renewables, including removing financial incentives for solar-power production, the Conservative government has expanded fracking for shale gas.[4]

In 2012, the government established the Office of Unconventional Gas and Oil with the explicit aim of 'develop[ing] the shale gas industry in the UK'. Shale is a sedimentary rock from which oil and gas can be extracted via a liquid pressure process known as hydraulic fracturing (fracking). In 2013, UK Chancellor of the Exchequer and Bilderberg Group member George Osborne 'announced support to encourage investment in onshore oil and gas, including shale gas, by halving the tax rate on early profits'. Citing British Geological Survey data, the government boasts that the Bowland-Hodder shale-gas site holds 1,300 trillion cubic feet of gas. Instead of relying on photovoltaics (solar), hydropower and windfarms, the government says that shale gas obtained by fracking will solve the UK's energy needs. Between 20 and 40 potential shale gas sites will be explored as a result of the Infrastructure Act 2015, which allows companies greater access. The government has also consulted on 'new standard rules permits, which reduce the time it takes to get a permit for certain types of low-risk oil and gas activities to up to four weeks'.[5]

Trump is agnostic about climate change and found a natural ally in the neoliberal, rightwing British Conservative government.

Some key statistics on pollution

Each year, human beings release approximately 40 billion tonnes of carbon dioxide (CO_2) into the atmosphere. According to NASA's Earth Observatory, 8.4 billion tonnes are attributed to the burning of fossil fuels, primarily coal, gas and oil. The European Commission and Netherlands Environmental

Assessment Agency list the ten most polluting countries (including the EU as a whole and each of its member states): China, the US, the EU, India, Russia, Japan, Germany, South Korea, Canada and Brazil. When measured in terms of per-capita emissions, the US and Canada are far ahead, with each person emitting an average of over 15 tonnes of CO_2 per annum ('carbon footprint'). This is a result of commuting, consumption, domestic energy use, leisure and travel. In more rural, less individually consumptive societies, like China and India, individuals have smaller carbon footprints.[6]

The EU's global emissions roughly correlate to per-capita emissions. This can be attributed to Europe's mild climate (excluding Scandinavia), the use of cleaner fuels and the offshoring of intensive industry to poorer countries. The biggest polluters in the Global South (Brazil, China, India) still have low per-capita emissions compared with rich countries. By far the least polluting continent is Africa, with Algeria, Egypt, Nigeria and South Africa its highest emitters. It is also worth remembering that the Majority World serves as a provider of resources, including oil and other raw materials for rich countries. Factories and assembly plants that use a lot of energy often produce goods for export to Europe and North America, making shipping and air transport big CO_2 emitters.[7]

China's CO_2 emissions are now twice that of the US, having equalled them just 10 years ago. Emissions of CO_2 in China are largely due to the use of coal and are disproportionately greater than the US because of the size of its population (there are 1.3 billion Chinese compared to 317 million Americans). Despite having a quarter of China's population, American per-capita CO_2 emissions are nearly triple those of China. Consumption is a major factor. The average Chinese person uses 3,500 kilowatts of energy per hour (kWh) compared with the average American, who uses over 12,000. In China, there are 128 motor vehicles per 1,000 people. In the US, there are 809 per 1,000. Food consumption is another factor. The average daily calorie intake in China is 2,900. In the US, it is 3,750.[8]

In the 1980s, China adopted US-style privatization programmes, agreeing to huge inflows of American capital. Within 20 years, China had equalled the US's record on annual

CO_2 emissions. It would seem that the more westernized countries become, the more likely they are to pollute. Statista estimates that by the year 2000, US corporations were investing $11.14 billion in China. By 2007, they were investing $29.71 billion. This leapt to $53.93 billion in 2008 and climbed to $65.77 billion by 2014. Much of the so-called investment is internal to US corporations, as companies looking for cheap labour outsource to China. For example, the trade journal *Manufacturing and Technology News* reports: 'Hundreds of major American corporations are shipping thousands of jobs overseas', where workers' rights, pay and health and safety standards are lower. Plus, foreign countries offer huge tax breaks on foreign direct investment. Big companies and their subsidiaries and divisions that offshore production to China, Mexico and other poor countries with low environmental standards, include: AT&T, Boeing, General Dynamics, Hewlett Packard, IBM, International Paper, Kingston Technology, Motorola, Nordex, Rockwell Automation, Sony Pictures Imageworks, Staples, Tenneco Automotive and Tyco Electronics.[9]

However, the use of robotics and software means that more jobs can be relocated to the US ('onshored') in US tax havens.

By 2014, CO_2 accounted for 80.9 per cent of anthropogenic US greenhouse-gas emissions. The US Environmental Protection Agency (EPA), which has a terrible record on environmental protection, says that combustion (of coal, gas and oil) is the main human activity that releases CO_2. Electrical production, which uses coal combustion for its generation, accounts for 37 per cent of US CO_2 emissions. Transport comes a close second, at 31 per cent, which is where oil comes in, as most transport (cars, trucks, planes, ships) relies on petroleum. Industry is responsible for 15 per cent of emissions and residential/commercial activities for 10 per cent. Between 1990 and 2014, US CO_2 emissions increased by 9 per cent. EPA cites as ways of reducing emissions: energy efficiency (such as insulation, fuel efficiency and waste management), conservation (turning off appliances when not in use), fuel switching (using green technologies) and carbon capture.[10]

With this in mind, let's consider the record of the Obama-Clinton administration in the US on the fossil-fuels industry.

Hillary Clinton continues the trend

In the 2006 edition of her book *It Takes a Village*, originally published in 1996, Hillary Clinton makes a reference to climate change in the Introduction. She notes 'the threats posed by global climate change, catastrophic environmental events, and the spread of deadly diseases'. Apart from that, there are no references to 'climate change' or 'global warming' in the book.[11]

In her memoir, *Living History* (2003), Clinton also makes zero reference to 'global warming' or 'climate change'. She makes a few scattered references to the 'environment', with no commitments to policies and without giving any sense of her interest (or lack thereof) in the issue. For example: the Republicans wanted 'to abolish the Department of Education, make deep spending cuts in Medicare, Medicaid, education and the environment and slash tax credits for the working poor'. Republicans felt that budgets could be met 'only with deep reductions in education, environmental protection and health care programs'.[12]

Clinton used environmental issues as a weapon against governments who feared that US non-governmental organizations (NGOs) were engaged in subversion in their countries. For example, Clinton was asked by NGOs to attend political meetings against Slovakian Prime Minister Vladimír Mečiar, who was 'a throwback to the era of authoritarian regimes. He wanted to outlaw [NGOs], seeing them as threats to his rule'. Clinton goes on: 'My presence at the meeting... emboldened the participants to speak frankly about issues such as minority rights, environmental damage and flawed election procedures'.[13]

As First Lady, Clinton continues, 'I would emphasize issues relating to women, healthcare, education, human rights, the environment and grassroots efforts such as microcredit to jumpstart economies'. Clinton believed in a conspiracy of:

> ... an interlocking network of groups and individuals who want to turn the clock back on many of the advances our country has made, from civil rights and women's rights to consumer and environmental regulation, and they use all the tools at

their disposal – money, power, influence, media and politics – to achieve their ends.[14]

She also wrote that 'issues that mattered to voters' included 'federal help to reduce class size and to help with school construction, Social Security and health insurance reforms, better foster care and adoption practices and protection of the environment'.

Clinton considered the impeachment proceedings against her husband to be a conspiracy waged by those who were 'determined to sabotage the President's agenda on the economy, education, Social Security, healthcare, the environment and the search for peace in Northern Ireland, the Balkans and the Middle East – everything we, as Democrats, stood for'.

The only thing of substance Clinton had to say in her memoir regarding the environment is that First Lady Johnson [in the 1960s] 'began a beautification program that spread wildflowers along thousands of miles of US highways and enhanced our appreciation of the natural landscape. Through [her] advocacy, a generation of Americans learned new respect for the environment and were inspired to preserve it'. Clinton doesn't mention President Johnson's decimation of Vietnam from saturation bombing, destroying millions of acres of jungle and fields which may never recover.[15]

From these quotations, it is clear that 'the environment' is a generic, 'progressive' term of little substance used by Clinton in her packaging of social issues.

By the time Clinton wrote *Hard Choices* (2014), climate change had become a serious issue and she devotes an entire chapter to US policies on energy and the environment. The following quotations are taken from that chapter.[16]

The chapter begins with an attack on China. Clinton and President Obama 'knew that the only way to achieve a meaningful agreement on climate change was for leaders of the nations emitting the most greenhouse gases to sit down together and hammer out a compromise, especially the United States and China'. Clinton discusses her desire to use renewables as a way of getting so-called developing economies to 'leapfrog' from fossil fuels. Clinton goes on to say that in

2008, she and Obama declared climate change to be a serious issue. Clinton and Obama tried to 'incentiv[ize]' renewable usage via cap-and-trade and other schemes, she says. Obama and Clinton were eager, but the Senate was reluctant. Even more reluctant, she claims, were other nations.

Clinton employed Todd Stern as her Special Envoy for Climate Change to help with the UN negotiations at the Copenhagen summit in December 2009. The goal was to sign the UN Framework Convention on Climate Change. The US's goal, says Clinton, was to convince 'China, Japan, South Korea, and Indonesia to adopt better climate policies'. The Chinese government, says Clinton, 'was refusing to commit to any binding international agreements on emissions'. Throwing India into the mix, Clinton criticizes 'these rapidly developing countries' which 'insisted on playing by the old rules and pumping massive amounts of carbon into the atmosphere'. However, she also reiterates that per capita, the US is (or was at the time of writing) the biggest polluter.

After the failure of other countries to compromise, says Clinton, the Copenhagen meeting stalled until the next one in 2015. In 2012, Clinton announced the Climate and Clean Air Coalition to tackle the big polluters, black carbon dust, hydrofluorocarbons and methane. The Coalition is mostly aimed at poor countries, including Bangladesh, Colombia, Ghana, Malaysia and Nigeria, but also Canada, Mexico and Scandinavia.

China is 'hungry for energy and excited by the prospects of new shipping routes that could cut the travel time between ports in Shanghai and Hong Kong and markets in Europe by thousands of miles'. The key region is the Arctic. We 'need to prevent this latter-day gold rush from overwhelming the Arctic's fragile ecosystem and accelerating climate change'. There's little chance of that now with Trump in office. Clinton concludes: 'If we let the Arctic turn into the Wild West, the health of the planet and our security would be at risk.' By this, Clinton means that US corporate profits would be at risk. Gas is less harmful than coal, says Clinton, who suggests that domestically the US should reduce coal emissions and replace them with gas.

Clinton as Secretary of State: countries as 'laboratories'

Fracking (hydraulic fracturing) is a deep-drilling process in which gas and oil is extracted from subterranean shale. The rocks are fractured by high-pressure liquids. The process can pollute drinking water because natural and human-made chemicals can spill into aquifers during drilling, pressure application and extraction. Fracking can also cause earthquake-like tremors. Despite her words about balancing the US's supposed economic needs with non-binding commitments to reduce emissions, and despite her efforts to pressure 'developing' countries to reduce emissions, Clinton championed fracking abroad.

An unclassified cable from 2009 reveals Clinton's true interest in 'unconventional' energy, in particular shale gas. 'Recent technological advances in natural gas production could have a significant impact on international energy security and climate change.' She refers to shale gas as 'one of the most quickly expanding trends in US oil and gas exploration, with significant international potential. The Department [of State] and Washington interagency community are working to assess the international potential for shale gas development, and where USG [US government] outreach efforts could be best directed.'[17]

It goes on: 'The Department is asking that posts assess the state of shale gas development and/or potential for development in their host country and report their findings to Washington.' The cable discusses using shale gas as a geopolitical weapon against India and China and a way of securing the EU's energy requirements: 'Significant potential for production of shale gas and other forms of unconventional gas (coal bed methane and tight gas) exists abroad, and could have important implications, particularly in China and India (climate change) and Europe (energy security).' Clinton adds: 'The US Geological Survey is beginning to work with foreign partners on mapping the potential of shale gas, and we are looking at how we can assist them with this work'.[18]

Libya has the largest known oil reserves in Africa, as well as significant gas reserves. From 2005 to 2009 David Goldwyn was director of the US-Libya Business Association, whose members include Chevron, ExxonMobil and Marathon. Goldwyn also worked in the Department of Energy under Bill Clinton. In 2005, he and Jan Kalicki (of Chevron) authored a book entitled *Energy and Security: Toward a New Foreign Policy Strategy*, which advocates fracking. In 2009, Clinton appointed Goldwyn as Special Envoy for Energy Affairs. Unclassified embassy cables reveal that US State Department planners feared that fracking was getting a bad reputation and 'need[s] to find advocates outside of industry'. It goes on to note 'Goldwyn's suggestions regarding the need for additional fact-based, third party research, trends on energy efficiency improvements, and increasing visibility and accessibility of more positive news stories'.[19]

In 2010, Goldwyn announced that Clinton's State Department had formed the Global Shale Gas Initiative, a body designed to push fracking on other countries. The initial meeting of the US Energy Association included Chevron, ConocoPhillips, ExxonMobil and Shell. The organization's first international meeting took place in August of that year and barred media involvement, even to the point where participating countries were not revealed to the public. The State Department's Chuck Ashley wrote that 'Poland is a laboratory for testing whether US success in developing shale gas can be repeated in a different country [to the US], with different shale, and different regulatory environment'. Polish demonstrators, including the group Occupy Chevron, were successful in getting the US energy giant to halt operations in 2015.[20]

The US sold fracking to Poland as a way of breaking the latter's energy dependence on Russia. Halliburton, a company once led by former Vice President Dick Cheney, garnered a reputation in Iraq for profiting from the US-British war, as did dozens of other companies. In particular, Halliburton won 'cost-plus' contracts, meaning that it was financially beneficial for the company to waste time and money because expenses were paid, plus interest; hence the enormous cost and waste involved in 'rebuilding' Iraq (which never happened). Halliburton drilled the first fracking well in Poland. In defence of Halliburton and against the protesters, Poland's state-owned energy company cried: 'Don't put out the flame of hope'. Poland's fracking concessions included nearly a third of its land mass.[21]

In 2011, Clinton inaugurated the Bureau of Energy Resources, stating: 'You can't talk about our economy or foreign policy without talking about energy.' When Clinton resigned to run for the office of President, the Global Shale Gas Initiative was changed to the Unconventional Gas Technical Engagement Program.[22]

In that year, Bulgaria signed a five-year contract with Chevron. Worth $68 million, the deal reportedly granted Chevron the right to frack millions of acres. Anti-fracking demonstrators greeted Clinton's 2012 visit with placards reading, 'Stop fracking with our water' and 'Chevron go home'. In response, the Bulgarian parliament voted for a moratorium on fracking. Chevron also signed a deal to frack 2,700 square kilometres in Romania. Following protests, the Romanian parliament issued a draft bill proposing to ban fracking. The US Ambassador to Romania intervened to push the Romanian government on the concessions. He said: 'The Romanians were just sitting on the leases, and Chevron was upset. So I intervened'. The moratorium never happened.[23]

Clinton responded to these cases of direct democracy by organizing a team of fracking 'experts' to convince the respective governments to go ahead with the operations. Clinton's Special Envoy for Energy in Eurasia, Richard Morningstar, was sent to both Bulgaria and Romania to meet with top officials and promote fracking on national radio, where he said that fracking could reduce gas prices fivefold. Morningstar's campaign worked, for a while.[24]

Hampering the Copenhagen climate summit

The Obama administration's policies continued to worsen the climate crisis.

A paper published by the UN states that in the 1980s, an 'international consensus' emerged that states should work towards a legally binding agreement on climate change and related issues. The first step was the establishment of the Intergovernmental Panel on Climate Change by the UN World

Meteorological Organization and the UN Environmental Programme in 1988. At the Second World Climate Conference in 1990 'the United States... did not want to be subject to any obligation to reduce emissions'. The environment news website *Grist* reminds us that the Democrat-controlled Senate ratified the UN Framework Convention on Climate Change in 1992, but that the agreement is 'legally nonbinding'. It merely commits signatories to attend regular international meetings.[25]

What about the Copenhagen summit in 2009, the failure of which was blamed on China? Under President Bill Clinton, the US military announced a policy called Full Spectrum Dominance. The plan envisages global militarization 'to protect US interests and investment' and includes an element called 'info dominance'. As part of 'info dominance', the mega surveillance organization, the National Security Agency (NSA), tries to access every phone call, email, website, smartphone and even baby monitors with the aim of listening to, recording, storing and analysing all communications on Planet Earth. Numerous whistleblowers and journalists – long before WikiLeaks and Edward Snowden – exposed this, but it was only the Assange-Snowden leaks that for some reason made an impact.[26]

The US relies heavily on the UK's RAF Menwith Hill station in Yorkshire, run by Britain's GCHQ. British signals intelligence (SIGINT) reportedly covers the whole of Europe.[27]

The NSA/GCHQ spied on the Copenhagen climate summit 2009. 'According to some observers, the spying may have contributed to the Americans getting their way in the negotiations', says Denmark's newspaper, *Information*, which broke the story. When Hillary Clinton was Secretary of State, the NSA's division S17 for Economic and Global Issues was tasked with spying on the communications of all the Convention's member states negotiators 'to provide policymakers with unique, timely, and valuable insights into key countries' preparations and goals', to quote from the leaked documents. The leaked documents note that 'SIGINT has already alerted policymakers to anticipate specific foreign pressure on the United States and has provided insights into planned actions on this issue by key nations and leaders'.[28]

The newspaper reminds us that 'the Americans had refused to commit to the [Kyoto] protocol'. Interestingly, the newspaper reveals that Denmark's Under-Secretary of State, Bo Lidegaard, had overseen the drafting of an agreement 'which favored American interests'. The Danish Minister for Climate and Energy, Connie Hedegaard, who went on to become the EU Commissioner for Climate Action, allegedly 'stress[ed] the importance of making sure that the Americans did not see the US-friendly Danish text', as this would encourage the US negotiators to seek even more concessions.[29]

As Hillary Clinton admits in her 2014 book, the US goal at the Copenhagen summit was to pressure 'developing' countries into making the biggest commitments to emissions reductions. *Information* concludes that the US committed to reduce emissions by up to 6 per cent, despite the UN recommending that states reduce by a minimum of 25 per cent.[30]

The Copenhagen summit of 2009 was widely reported as a failure and this was attributed to China's intransigence. However, as the leaks show, that is not the full story. Known as the 'Danish text', an agreement drafted by EU members without input from the US was leaked in December 2009. The draft text infuriated so-called developing countries because it made it clear that they would be asked to make disproportionate concessions by the powerful countries, while the rich countries carried on polluting, almost as normal.[31]

Climate issues and the Clinton presidential campaign

In February 2016, the Democratic National Committee did a U-turn on accepting contributions from federally registered lobbyists. Clinton's presidential campaign in 2016 received donations from the fossil-fuel industries, including maximum allowable donations from individuals, 'bundles' and contributions from organizations. So-called Political Action Committees (PACs and super-PACS) working in favour of Clinton's campaign received $4 million from the fossil-fuel industry. Greenpeace USA writes: 'Hillary Clinton's campaign and the Super PAC supporting her have received more than $6.9 million.' Donations to the Clinton Campaign Committee included over $300,000 from individual donors linked to oil, gas and coal companies. Fossil-fuel lobbyists, including those who had made bundled contributions, donated $2.65 million.[32]

Greenpeace asked Clinton to sign the following pledge:

> By 'fossil-fuel interests' we mean companies whose primary business is the extraction, processing and sale of coal, oil or gas. The pledge means that a candidate's campaign will adopt a policy to not knowingly accept any contributions from company PACs, registered lobbyists that work on behalf of the company, or top executives.

Clinton refused.[33]

In the late 1970s, James Black was employed by the world's biggest oil company, Exxon. After building climate models incorporating the impact of CO_2 emissions, Black informed the company that continued fossil-fuel usage could raise global temperatures by between 2°C and 3°C, increases that are generally considered tipping points for catastrophic changes. Exxon responded by keeping its internal scientific findings a secret and by publicly financing climate-change-denial propaganda to the tune of $30 million, including helping to establish the Global Climate Coalition, a thinktank designed to challenge climate-change science. It successfully lobbied Bill Clinton's government not to sign the Kyoto Protocol on reducing emissions in 1998. An Exxon lobbyist, Theresa Fariello, donated $21,200 in bundles to Hillary Clinton's presidential campaign in 2016.[34]

The fossil-fuel lobby has links to many individuals, companies and financiers. Mary Streett, of Britain's oil giant BP, gave the maximum allowable donation ($2,700). Streett's sister, Stephanie, is Executive Director of the William J Clinton Foundation and former Executive Director of the Bill, Hillary and Chelsea Clinton Foundation. The Podesta Group also lobbied on behalf of BP over numerous issues, including the Gulf of Mexico oil disaster.[35]

The former Ukrainian government minister, Nikolai Zlochevskyi, controls Brociti Investments, based in Cyprus. The firm owns Burisma Holdings, a private natural gas and uranium mining company based in Ukraine. A lobbyist for Burisma, David Leiter, was a Clinton bundler and lobbyist for Exxon, and is a former Senate chief of staff to Secretary of State John Kerry. In 2014 Hunter Biden, son of the then Vice-President Joe Biden, joined Burisma Holdings. Another Burisma board member, Devon Archer, donated $2,700 to the Clinton campaign.[36] Three more mining groups – Arch Coal, Westmoreland Coal and Britain's Rio Tinto – also began making contributions to the Clinton campaign.

The lobbying continued. Former Democrat Representative Dick Gephardt's firms, including Ameren Services, Peabody Energy and Prairie State, also lobbied. Ben Klein of Heather Podesta and Associates lobbied for Oxbow Carbon on issues including petcoke, a refining by-product, as did a number of liquefied natural gas (LNG) companies: Freeport LNG, LNG Allies, Dominion Resources, Oregon LNG, Exxon and Cheniere Energy, to name just some. Obama's former energy advisor, Heather Zichal, joined the board of Cheniere Energy.[37]

Specializing in 'government relations and public affairs', Forbes-Tate Partners lobbied for the Hess Corporation, North Dakota's third-largest oil producer, to ensure oil-transport rail cars. Former Hess executive Lynn Helms was North Dakota's oil and gas regulator at the Department of Mineral Resources. Hillary Clinton's rationale for opposing the Keystone Oil Pipeline System in Canada and the United States (see the next section below) was that fixing rail-car tracks would create jobs. Former Democrat Representative for Texas Martin Frost lobbied Clinton's campaign for the Domestic Energy Producers Alliance. Martin Durbin of the American Natural Gas Association, which became part of the American Petroleum Institute, also lobbied; as did Elizabeth Gore of WPX, a fracking company.[38]

Clinton and the Keystone XL pipeline

Between 2008 and 2009, the US State Department authorized the TransCanada corporation to build a pipeline from the tar sands of Alberta, Canada, to hubs in the US state of Nebraska. The pipeline would stretch for nearly 1,180 miles (1,888 km).

The proposed pipeline is called Keystone XL. Other Keystone pipelines run by TransCanada already span 3,000 miles (4,800 km). In 2015, however, Obama denied the requisite permit for the Keystone XL pipeline. TransCanada believes that under Chapter 11 of the North American Free Trade Agreement it is entitled to compensation for financial losses incurred by the cancellation of the project; the corporation claims that it and related organizations invested 'billions' in the project, including land leases.[39]

As Secretary of State, Clinton instead approved a pipeline by a rival company, Enbridge. Enbridge is a Canadian energy delivery company. In 2010, numerous environmental groups filed a law suit against Clinton and others. They were the Sierra Club, the Minnesota Center for Environmental Advocacy, the Indigenous Environmental Network and the National Wildlife Federation. They claimed that Clinton and others had violated the National Environmental Policy Act 'by issuing permits to build and operate an oil pipeline – the Alberta Clipper Pipeline... based on an inadequate Environmental Impact Statement'. The environmental groups aimed to prevent Clinton and her businesses from continuing construction of the Alberta Clipper Pipeline.[40]

The pipeline was designed to take oil from the same place as the Keystone pipeline – Hardisty, Alberta (Canada) – and then deliver it to Wisconsin (US).

Clinton's presidential campaign, 'Hillary for America' received money from the following groups or from individuals related to or acting on behalf of: American Fuel and Petro-chemical Manufacturers, American Natural Gas Association, American Petroleum Institute, Arch Coal, BP, Cheniere, Chesapeake, Chevron, ConocoPhilips, Domestic Energy Producers Alliance, Duke Energy, Energy Future Holdings, ExxonMobil, Freeport LNG Expansion, Lario Oil and Gas, Oxbow Carbon, Peabody Energy and Statoil. Note that Clinton's campaign took money from individuals associated with Trans-Canada's rival, Enbridge.[41]

There is no suggestion that money from Enbridge directly influenced Clinton or her State Department's decision to cancel the Keystone XL pipeline in favour of Enbridge pipelines. Nevertheless, in 2007 permits were granted by the Bush administration for the construction of pipelines by Enbridge and permits for TransCanada were cancelled.

Gung-ho for GMOs

When Hillary Clinton was a lawyer in Arkansas at Rose Law Firm, the company reportedly represented Monsanto, one of the world's biggest producers of genetically modified organisms (GMOs). Clinton's campaign manager for Iowa, Jerry Crawford, was a lobbyist for Monsanto. GMO producer Dow Chemical gave the Clinton Foundation between $1 million and $5 million. Monsanto (now part of Bayer) gave the Foundation between $500,000 and $1 million.[42]

In 2010, the Obama administration launched Feed the Future, an initiative designed to push US-EU insurance, chemical fertilizers and genetically modified foods on poor countries, mostly African. Or, as the website puts it: 'Feed the Future agencies work hand-in-hand with partner countries to develop their agriculture sectors and break the vicious cycle of poverty and hunger'. Partner countries include Bangladesh, Cambodia, Ethiopia, Ghana, Guatemala, Haiti, Honduras, Kenya, Liberia, Malawi, Mali, Mozambique, Nepal, Rwanda, Senegal, Tajikistan, Tanzania, Uganda and Zambia. Partner businesses include Monsanto and the insurance giant, Swiss Re. Clinton was Secretary of State at the time.[43]

In 2011, Feed the Future reported that Dr Rajiv Shah, administrator of the US Agency for International Development (USAID) 'gathered with the CEOs of [Anglo-Dutch company] Unilever and Monsanto to support the [World Economic Forum's] global framework'. In 2012, Feed the Future 'forged more than 660 public-private partnerships... and increased the value of agricultural and rural loans by more than $150 million'. According to Clinton's successor, John Kerry, Feed the Future has 'provided loans to farmers, both women and men; and forged public-private partnerships that catalyse lasting economic growth. Our partners are also rising to the challenge, with US-based non-governmental organizations pledging over $1 billion and global and African private-sector companies pledging over $3.7 billion.' Part of the programme includes 'broadening the investment base for food security and nutrition', including GMOs.[44]

Bilateral FTAs – and all the potential threats to sovereignty that go with them – are the framework through which Feed the Future projects are finalized. The US Trade Representative 'advances work on trade and investment policy, including trade facilitation and other efforts to reduce barriers to efficient markets consistent with international obligations' at the World Trade Organization, says the Feed the Future report of 2013. It does so 'through bilateral discussions such as Trade and Investment Framework Agreements, and through free-trade agreements'.[45]

Trump and his team hope that such deals can be used to push GMOs, toxic pesticides and low-grade meats on European nations.

In 2013, Feed the Future reported on its Research Strategy, which places 'a strong emphasis on developing high-yielding, climate-resilient cereals' – in other words, GMOs. This includes the Water Efficient Maize for Africa (WEMA) project. Feed the Future describes WEMA as '[a] unique public-private partnership focused on developing drought-tolerant and pest-resistant tropical maize for Eastern and Southern Africa'. It involves 'the Monsanto Company, and national agricultural research systems... in Kenya, Uganda, Tanzania, Mozambique and South Africa'. It is also supported by USAID, the Bill and Melinda Gates Foundation and the Howard G Buffett Foundation, Howard being the son of Warren 'class warfare' Buffett. The website boasts that maize varieties are being modified with 'insect-resistant "Bt" genes'.[46]

Bt cotton is a genetically modified maize that contains a soil bacterium, *Bacillus thuringiensis*. It is produced by Monsanto and its objective is to save maize from the destructive bollworm insect.

Clinton understands that the public tends to be suspicious of GMOs. '"Genetically modified" sounds Frankensteinish. "Drought resistance" sounds really – something you want. So how do you create a different vocabulary to talk about what it is you're trying to help people do?' Clinton said this in 2014, at a paid speaking engagement with the Biotechnology Industry (now Innovation) Organization (BIO). BIO's members include at least three Monsanto subsidiaries.[47]

The February 2016 Federal Election Commission report shows that Jerry Crawford of Iowa's Crawford & Mauro Law firm bundled $151,727 for Clinton's campaign ending in December 2015. Monsanto, the chemicals giant, is named as a client of Crawford's firm, which reportedly made $60,000 lobbying for Monsanto. Monsanto lobbyist Steve Elmendorf reportedly bundled $20,295 for the 'Hillary for America' campaign in the last quarter of 2015. Elmendorf works for the Grocery Manufacturers Association, which actively opposes GMO labelling laws.[48]

Clinton versus activists

In September 2015, a questioner at the Building Trades Union complained to Clinton that 'the Sierra Club won't support any natural gas'. They were hoping to find a friend in the Democratic Party. Clinton replied: 'I want to defend natural gas', in opposition to her Democratic rival, Bernie Sanders. 'I wanted to defend repairing and building the pipelines we need to fuel our economy. I want to defend fracking under the right circumstances... I'm already at odds with the most organized and wildest [environmental groups]' over this position, Clinton continued. 'They come to my rallies and they yell at me... They say, "Will you promise never to take any fossil fuels out of the earth ever again?" No. I won't promise that. Get a life, you know?'[49]

Once Sanders had been defeated, Clinton's speechwriters dropped direct references to climate change from her speeches and debates. After analysing speech transcripts, Climate Home, a website dedicated to news about climate change, found that, post-Sanders, Clinton referred to climate change in only 20 per cent of her public addresses. 'During the last six months of Clinton's primary campaign against Sanders, the transcript log of her speeches shows she was talking about climate change at one out of every two speeches she gave', says Climate Home. In 38 speeches between July and September 2016, 'Clinton mentioned climate change specifically eight times. Just once every five public addresses'. On 'the environment' in general, Clinton's position was even worse. 'In the 78 speeches for which Clinton's campaign have logged transcripts in 2016, she mentions the word in just four'.[50]

6 Fossil fuels: 'Exploitation should be guaranteed'

How the Obama administration allowed oil exports for the first time in over four decades. This interested Europe's elites, who are worried by their energy dependence on Russia.

As a result of President Obama's deregulation of the shale gas and oil industries, the US became the world's leading energy producer in 2014. As domestic consumption exceeds production, the US does not yet need to export, particularly in an oversupplied global market. According to a paper by the European Parliament: 'Industry lobbies are behind... moves' to lift the ban on oil and gas exports. They do not wish to supply an undervalued market, but rather set monopoly prices. By 2015, the US was importing 9.4 million barrels a day of petroleum from 88 countries. Seventy-eight per cent of these imports were crude petroleum. The top five source countries for US oil imports are: Canada, Saudi Arabia, Venezuela, Mexico and Colombia.[1]

In 2015, the US produced 4.7 million barrels of oil a day. Until December 2015, the US did not export oil but now wants to export to Europe, which currently imports most of its oil from Russia, Norway, Nigeria, Saudi Arabia and Kazakhstan.[2]

Europe's energy needs

According to its own website, the European Union relies on the US to secure global markets and supply lines for its energy imports. 'More than half of the EU-28's energy comes from countries outside the EU.' Without its own military, the EU relies on the US-led NATO and on the militarism of Britain which is the only EU member state to meet its two per cent of GDP military spending obligation. Britain has particularly strong military relations – resulting in human rights abuses – with Nigeria (where Shell operates) and Saudi Arabia (which operates a state-owned oil company), supplying the Saudis with military hardware worth billions of dollars per annum.[3]

The EU's energy statistics website goes on to note that: 'Concerns about the security of supply from Russia were further heightened by the conflict in Ukraine... There are a number of ongoing initiatives to develop gas pipelines between Europe and its eastern and southern neighbours' – much to the chagrin of the US which seeks to dominate supply lines. 'These include the Nord Stream (between Russia and the EU via the Baltic Sea) which became operational in November 2011 and the Trans-Adriatic Pipeline (connecting Turkey to Italy through Greece and Albania to bring gas from the Caspian Sea region to the EU)'.[4]

By revenue, the world's five largest energy companies are: Saudi Aramco, Sinopec, China National Petroleum Corporation, Petrochina and ExxonMobil. Only one is a US company (Exxon), though many would argue that without US and British weapons and military training, the Saudis and their oil economy would collapse. Also in the top ten are: Royal Dutch Shell, Kuwait Petroleum Corporation, BP, Total SA and Lukoil, with Eni following in 11th place. From this we see that Britain and Europe seek to maintain the importance of their oil and gas (Total is French and Eni Italian) within the context of a growing China and Russia (Lukoil and Gazprom).[5]

The EU was hoping to include an oil and gas chapter in the TTIP deal in order to regulate US imports. Former State Department law specialist Keith J Benes writes of the EU's insistence on the inclusion of an energy chapter in the agreement. 'The United States has not outright opposed such a chapter, but has indicated skepticism that it is necessary.' Battling a united Europe, the United States 'has to wrestle with restrictions on crude oil exports' coming from the EU 'and the potential strong domestic political opposition to relaxing them'. Benes goes on to note that, horror of horrors, the EU supports reducing fossil-fuel usage and 'faces becoming entangled in the environmental controversies around the rapidly expanding oil and gas production in North America', such as fracking in the US and tar-sand extraction in Canada.[6]

Further noting their opposition to the current form of the multilateral TTIP draft, the US Chamber of Commerce writes that 'the Obama administration should allow unfettered exports of [liquefied natural gas] to higher-priced markets in Asia, Europe and elsewhere'. The website continues: 'Barring any LNG exports would violate the free-trade commitments that the US has made as a leading member of the Geneva-based World Trade Organization.'[7]

But European businesses want to import US energy. By 2014, nearly 70 per cent of the EU's natural gas imports came from Russia and Norway, as did 40 per cent of oil imports. For this reason, Europe's politicians want to diversify supply. Other EU oil suppliers include Nigeria, Saudi Arabia and Kazakhstan. Seventy per cent of the EU's solid fuels (liquid gas, coal) came from Russia, Colombia and the US. Europe's dependence on energy imports has grown in recent decades, though the ex-Soviet states, including Estonia, Poland and Romania, rely less on imports compared with the rest of the EU.[8]

With Britain leaving the EU and the US exporting for the first time in 40 years, the European Commission hoped to use the two countries to diversify supplies and strengthen its own energy security.

Oil: 'eliminating existing limits' continues to hold sway

Facing massive lobbying from US energy firms, the European Commission sought to 'eliminate existing limits' on the extraction, production and sale of energy and materials; fracking was not ruled out. 'The government of each EU member country is responsible for deciding whether to allow shale-gas production in their country. Nothing in TTIP could limit this sovereign right of each EU country'. A similar document notes: 'Once exploitation is permitted... non-discriminatory access for exploitation... should be guaranteed by regulatory commitments.' The Commission has been pushing for a TTIP energy chapter in order to guarantee its energy 'security' in the face of instability in Ukraine – an instability arguably resulting from Anglo-American threats against Ukraine's neighbour, Russia.[9]

One barrel of oil consists of 159 litres. Each day, 96 million barrels of oil and liquid fuels are consumed worldwide (35 billion barrels a year). By 2014, the top five Western oil companies alone were worth over $300 billion: Shell ($92.3 billion), ExxonMobil ($87.2 billion), BP ($75 billion), Chevron ($46 billion) and ConocoPhillips ($11.8 billion). The US Bureau of Labor Statistics divides oil and gas sector employment into three categories: drilling (which employs 90,000 individuals), extraction (193,000) and support (286,000). Despite there being 93 billionaires in the global oil and energy sector, 'oil and gas exploration workers' in the US 'just became a little more like the average US worker', wrote journalist Tom DiChristopher in 2015, reporting on 60,500 layoffs that year. Extractors who survive the layoffs face a significant chance of death or serious injury. According to the US Department of Labor, between 2003 and 2010, 823 oil and gas extractors died on the job – 'a fatality rate seven times greater than the rate for all US industries'.[10]

It is not just drilling and extraction that make oil a dangerous commodity. US President Barack Obama said that 'no challenge poses a greater threat to future generations than climate change'. The White House says that 'taking steps to reduce carbon pollution presents an enormous opportunity to strengthen the economy, drive innovation, and create new jobs'. The Obama administration – with less than a year left in office – pledged to increase 'clean' transportation investments by 50 per cent, reduce CO_2 emissions and 'cut oil consumption'.[11]

This sounds very nice. The reality is somewhat different. Obama authorized more oil extraction than any other president in the past 40 years. CNN Money reports: 'Under Obama, the steady drop in US oil production which had occurred virtually unchecked since 1971 has been reversed.' The article goes on to note the annual rise in crude production 'every year' since Obama took office in 2009. Obama transformed the US into the world's largest producer, overtaking its (and Britain's) close ally, the Saudi dictatorship. The article points to hydraulic fracturing (fracking) as the main reason for the sudden interest. The technology has 'unlocked' the oil and shale gas that was previously unobtainable and, consequently, investment in US oil capacity has increased, driving demand. It also sounds nice that the bulk of drilling has occurred on private not public land, until we read the Sierra Club's Athan Manuel, who points out: 'It's harder to regulate on private land.' This means that private extractors can flout regulation. Commenting on the decision to reverse 40 years of domestic oil production policy, Tom Kloza, chief analyst at Oil Price Information Service, says: 'It's capitalism at work.'[12]

Well, not quite. It's more like socialism for the rich and capitalism for the poor, to quote a popular phrase. As Chevron put it in its letter on TTIP to the US government, 'Robust investment protections enable Chevron, and companies like us, to put our capital at risk in order to provide the energy required to fuel economic growth and energy security.'[13]

According to the Center for Responsive Politics, the fossil-fuel industry spent under $72 million between 1998 and 2005 lobbying Congress. In 2006, the figure crept above the $72-million mark. By 2009, when Obama was in power, industry lobbying had leapt to nearly $180 million and stayed around the $144-million mark even after the BP Deepwater Horizon catastrophe, which killed 11 oil workers, released 4.9 million barrels of oil across 68,000 square miles (176,000 sq km) of ocean, led to a tenfold increase in dolphin deaths and a fourfold increase in strandings, not to mention the killing and injuring of untold numbers of other marine life and species.

International Business Times reports that the G20 nations – the rich countries which account for about 85 per cent of global GDP – spend $452 billion of public money a year on fossil-fuel subsidies. The US government alone provided $20.5 billion to oil, gas and coal producers. The *Business Times* article concludes that, since Obama took office, subsidies had 'increased by 35 per cent'. After BP's catastrophic 'spill', subsidies on clean-ups allowed BP to claim a $9.9-billion tax reduction. The subsidy cycle creates more demand, as *The McKinsey Quarterly* explains that 'subsidies... led to higher consumption than if people had to pay the market price'.[14]

Sitting on renewables

In 2013, European trade officials briefed 11 energy companies, including BP, ExxonMobil and Shell. Documents obtained by the *Guardian* suggest that European negotiators asked oil companies (including refineries) to help draft an energy chapter for TTIP. BusinessEurope was offered points of contact with negotiators in the US Departments of Energy and State.[15]

Chevron's 2013 letter to the Office of the US Trade Representative states: 'Chevron strongly supports this initiative... We urge governments to complete their domestic consultations promptly and begin these negotiations as soon as possible'. Chevron boasts of its upstream and downstream activities in Bulgaria, Denmark, France, Lithuania, the Netherlands, Norway, Poland, Romania and the UK, and of its 'significant discoveries' of energy reserves near Britain's Shetland Islands. 'Investment requires the strongest possible protection', says Chevron. 'We invest billions of dollars each year'. The global energy industry will invest $19 trillion to meet demand up to 2035. 'Investments, such as developing shale gas and tight resources in the United States and Europe, involve long-term commitments and substantial private capital', the company continues.[16]

The same letter says that 'Chevron was heartened by the... "competitive neutrality" [announcement] for private commercial enterprises and state-owned entities', which was agreed by the US and the EU in their statements issued in 2012 on Shared Principles for International Investment. In reality, there is no neutrality between the state and corporations. Big corporations cannot survive without the state and the state is heavily influenced by big corporations.[17]

The Trade in Services Agreement (TISA) is a secret TTIPesque multilateral draft text designed to promote more privatization and deregulation in the services sector, which by now accounts for about 80 per cent of US and UK GDPs. The draft text was leaked but, compared with TTIP and TPP, received little media attention.

'The Energy sector is an important and growing market in the global economy', says one of the leaked TISA Annexes.

The World Trade Organization and other agreements have 'struggled to capture this important market'. But the new age of bilateral globalization will do so – or will try to, at least. 'Energy is sensitive and related to issues of security/sovereignty', the document continues – hence the awesome scale of Anglo-American warfare in the energy-rich Middle East and North Africa. The aim of TISA is 'to encompass all services related to the exploration for and production of energy from renewable or non-renewable energy sources, as well as all delivery forms such as fuels, heat, and electrical energy'.[18]

Renewables? you may ask. Surely corporations are hell-bent on profit-maximization, of which oil and gas offer the safest market? This is true but, assuming that the documents were not leaked deliberately as part of a disinformation campaign, the renewables sector is a growing market which the big banks and fossil-fuel companies want to corner. They aim to sit on the technology, as they did in the 1980s and 1990s, to sell and lease it in periods of declining demand for fossil fuels: and of course to monopolize the budding market.

Oil and gas companies moved into the renewables sector in the 1980s, partly in response to the so-called price shocks of the 1970s. The big companies mainly researched doom-loop biofuels, including ethanol and algae feedstock. These energy sources are intensive compared to solar, hydro and wind power. Ethanol, for instance, requires the use of land, which affects food prices. In more recent years, BP and Total have moved into solar manufacturing, Shell into wind power, Chevron into geothermal energy and BP, Shell and Total into hydrogen fuel cells. As big oil lobbying increased on Capitol Hill, investments in renewables contracted.

In 2013, global capacity was 143 gigawatts of renewable energy compared to 141 gigawatts of fossil fuels.[19] Despite this, by 2013 renewables only accounted for just over 13 per cent of US domestic electrical production.[20]

The McKinsey Quarterly reports that, despite the drop in oil prices from 2014 to 2015, clean-technology companies did very well. In the previous decade, Chinese solar production destroyed many European and American green tech firms. However, 2014 saw a 17-per-cent increase in clean technology, with private equity investments rising 54 per cent. In the US, there is growth in green technology investments, with 12 gigawatts of renewable capacity installed by 2016, wind capacity up 10.9 per cent by the same year and solar up to possibly 18 per cent by 2040. 'The link between oil and renewables appears to be working', says the journal – which is bad for green tech because market forces continue to give big oil a licence to pollute.[21]

The TISA document spells out the oil and gas industries' plan to capture the green market, which is driven by the affordability of renewables, sector protection (such as tax credits and portfolio standards) and competition. In addition to the (perhaps ambitious) projections for green tech usage, oil prices for domestic consumers have fallen. Oil accounts for less than one per cent of power generation in the US and is mostly used for vehicles. If there are more cars on the road, as Trump envisions, there will be more oil, more pollution, more CO_2 and more climate chaos. If gas replaces coal as the number one power-generating fuel, it may be slightly cleaner for the environment, but a glut of cheap gas will hurt the renewables market.[22]

The wider energy context makes it clear that the worst aspects of TPP, TTIP and TISA will find their way into bilateral trade agreements on energy and transport unless activists organize against them on a scale similar to the anti-TTIP demonstrations.

7 Vehicles: Investor-State dispute settlements as 'gunboat diplomacy'

How corporations can now sue governments using trade law – and how the poor inevitably lose out as a consequence.

According to the European Commission, had the EU signed onto TTIP, EU exports outside the Single Market would have boosted sales of metal products, processed foods, chemicals, generic manufacturing goods, transport equipment and, crucially, motor vehicles (by an additional 41 per cent as compared with, say, processed foods at 9 per cent). For the good of the climate and air quality, exporting more gas-guzzling, polluting vehicles is precisely what we need to stop doing. As noted, there is nothing in TTIP requiring that exported vehicles meet strict environmental standards (for example, by specifying electric cars only). A similar bilateral deal between a post-Brexit UK and the Trump-led US, or a US-EU 'free trade' agreement could have similar or worse consequences. Despite there being no specific environmental provisions or enforcement mechanisms in TTIP, the general concerns raised by some EU representatives within their drafts of the text irked US business representatives.

Vehicles and pollution: 'market-based approaches'

In 2015, the US Environmental Protection Agency (EPA) strategically alleged that Germany's Volkswagen company (and others, including Audi and Porsche) had been violating the Clean Air Act by installing software to cheat emissions tests. Volkswagen stocks and shares plunged 20 per cent. Although this revealed actual malpractice by the car companies, it was arguably a way for the US to hurt European manufacturers and retailers in order to protect and boost its own car industry.[1]

The US move against Germany suggested that it was unhappy with the kinds of environmental obstacles Europe was erecting as part of the multilateral TTIP agreement. Article 1 of the TISA *Annex on Road Freight Transport and Related Logistics Services* states: 'This annex is aimed at liberalizing access by the Parties to each other's road freight transport and related logistics market in such a way to insure [sic] the existence of a sound international competition environment and smooth operation of carriage of goods'. Another Article states: 'No limitations shall be imposed on vehicles in transit and their drivers.' Had TISA been agreed or should similar treaties come to pass, the US could cite examples like the Volkswagen emissions scandal as justification for raising environmental tariffs against European freight and transport while taking European governments to arbitration panels for raising standards against US imports and operations.[2]

Article 5 of TISA states that 'Parties shall abolish and abstain from introducing any administrative and technical requirements and procedures which could constitute a disguised restriction or have discriminatory effects on the free supply of services in international transport', a category into which nationalization, health and safety testing and environmental issues may fall. A subsection of that Article states: 'When a Party transfers the management and operation of a public infrastructure for logistics services related to road freight transport, the competent authorities of each Party shall... rely generally on market-based approaches'.[3]

Brexit or not, Britain is literally paving the way for more car imports. Figures are not easy to come by, but the low estimates are that the Conservatives cut £28 billion ($36.7 billion) from public spending – including public transport – from 2010 to 2017. The poorest were hit the hardest, with £13 billion ($17 billion) cut from the most vulnerable. This plunged 500,000 children into poverty and reduced one million individuals to using food banks. Meanwhile, under its Action for Roads scheme, the Conservatives announced that, over ten years, £30 billion ($39.3 billion) will be spent upgrading the UK's roads, including constructing a tunnel around Stonehenge.[4]

Apparently missing the irony, the same edition of the *Sunday Express* newspaper carrying the story ran a smaller headline: 'New £2.3 billion [$3 billion] drive to improve UK's flood defence.' A year later, the same newspaper reported: 'Austerity cuts... could have cost the UK economy more than £1 billion [$1.3 billion] after flood defence plans went unfinished'. A freedom of information request filed by this author in 2015 revealed that a 'stakeholder group' called the Strategic Roads Reform Expert Group consulted with the government on the roads strategy. Not one organization represented the renewables or alternative energy sector. Instead, the group comprised, among others: the Automobile Association, the Confederation of British Industry, the Freight Transport Association and the Society of Motor Manufacturers and Traders.[5]

Why cars and oil dominate

In 2004, the US Chamber of Commerce published a lobbying document called *Top 10 Environmental Myths*, designed to relax politicians, policymakers and concerned industrialists about their decimation of the ecosystem on which all life depends. Myth Number 8 – 'Oil can easily be replaced by renewable energy' – is, according to the Chamber, countered by Fact Number 8: 'Oil is absolutely essential to all aspects of the American economy'. Note the use of the phrase 'all aspects'. In 2004, Professor Michael Klare predicted that a financial crisis would result from the invasion of Iraq, which was undertaken partly to increase US control over the global oil market. Several economists have demonstrated the link between oil prices, property value and financial market fluctuations in the build-up to the crash of 2008. The Chamber is not exaggerating when it says that 'all aspects' are reliant on oil. (In the real world there is no economic law which states that oil and other non-renewables have to dominate global markets.)[6]

Efforts to overcome what President George W Bush once called our 'addiction' to oil have been crushed over the years. As long ago as the late 19th century, investors from Britain,

France, Hungary and the Netherlands designed battery-powered cars and carriages. The first successful car powered by electricity was invented in 1890 by William Morrison. In 1898, Ferdinand Porsche developed the P1 electric car. Edison and Ford also worked on models. By 1915, 60 electric taxis were in use in New York. By the beginning of the 20th century, a third of all cars were electric, showing 'strong sales' over the next decade, according to the US Department of Energy. However, the Ford company then produced internal combustion engines that allowed petroleum-fuelled cars to be sold at a fraction of the cost. The discovery of oil in Texas made petroleum cheaper than electricity. In addition, the expansion of US roads required cars to have longer operating times, a service which petroleum could provide. Few Americans outside cities had access to electricity, yet petrol pumps were available to everyone.[7]

Another misfortune to befall the environment, human health and the 'clean' energy market was the so-called General Motors streetcar conspiracy. Between 1938 and 1950, the transportation company National City Lines (NCL) and its subsidiaries were acquired by Firestone Tire, General Motors, Mack Trucks, Phillips Petroleum and Standard Oil's subsidiary, Federal Engineering. This gave the corporations effective control over the tramlines of 25 cities. In 1948, the San Diego Electric Railway was bought by Western Transit Co before having its trams converted to petroleum-fuelled buses. The same happened to the Baltimore Streetcar system, which was bought by NCL. In 1949, Firestone et al were convicted by the Federal District Court in northern Illinois of conspiracy to monopolize the sale of buses (which relied on oil and tyres) over trams. Ironically, Baltimore is cited in a report by the Massachusetts Institute of Technology (MIT) as being one of the worst areas in the US for car pollution and early human mortality today.[8]

Cars, trucks and the human cost

There are 800 million cars in the world. According to Automotive Industry Solutions, there are 253 million cars and trucks in use in the US. There are 234 million cars on the roads of western Europe in a sector that employs 13 million people. The Union of Concerned Scientists reports that half of all carbon monoxide and nitrogen oxides and a quarter of aromatic hydrocarbons released each year can be attributed to transport. The Union further notes that much of the pollution could easily be reduced by clean vehicle-fuel technologies. The particulate matter emitted by vehicle exhausts (which is less than one-tenth the width of a human hair) is most dangerous to human health, as it penetrates the lungs.[9] It is not just the use of vehicles which causes pollution. The Union also points out that from design to manufacture to disposal, vehicle-related pollution is significant.

Ten per cent of current EU-US trade is with the automotive industry. Europe and the US capture 32 per cent of worldwide auto production and 35 per cent of global sales. The European Automobile Manufacturers Association (ACEA) boasts of its lobbying efforts, writing: 'Throughout the TTIP process, ACEA has been working actively with its US counterparts... to provide input to the authorities on both sides of the Atlantic. ACEA is also working closely on regulatory convergence with the Truck and Engine Manufacturers Association.' It also says that EU exports to the US could increase by 149 per cent by 2027. This, combined with non-tariff barrier reductions, would make the automotive industry account for over a third of total bilateral trade flow increases.[10]

One of the little-discussed factors in the commercial automotive industry is the car-to-density ratio. In poorer countries with huge populations, including Brazil, China and India, there are millions of cars because there are millions of people. However, per capita, private vehicle ownership is much lower than in rich countries. In other words, the more 'developed' a country is, the more affluent, the cheaper the products and the higher the owner-to-density ratio.[11]

The Massachusetts Institute of Technology (MIT) estimates that air pollution kills 200,000 Americans every year: about the same number of people worldwide who died in terror attacks over a 40-year period. MIT's Laboratory of Aviation and the Environment tracked emissions at ground-level, from industrial smokestacks, vehicles, railways and residential heating. Vehicle emissions alone kill 53,000 and power generators 52,000 people in the US annually. California has the worst air quality, with 21,000 persons dying prematurely each year. On average, sulphur, carbon monoxide and other pollutants shorten by a decade the lifespans of those affected. Researchers found that congestion is one of the reasons for large numbers of vehicle-related deaths. Fewer people are affected in less populated areas where traffic flow is reduced. Commercial and private pollution was highest in the Midwest, though particular hotspots were Atlanta, Chicago, Detroit, Philadelphia and Los Angeles.[12]

According to the World Health Organization (WHO), seven million people die each year round the world as a result of exposure to air pollution. This equates to one in eight global deaths. Air pollution is the single biggest environmental health risk and previous estimates have more than doubled. Indoor and outdoor pollution are linked to cancer, ischaemic (artery) heart disease and strokes. Poor and less-developed countries have the worst air quality, with particularly toxic air in South and East Asia and the Western Pacific. In those regions 3.3 million deaths are attributed to indoor pollution (including work-related air quality) and 2.6 million to outdoor pollution.[13]

Dr Flavia Bustreo, WHO's Assistant Director-General of Family, Women and Children's Health, says: 'Poor women and children pay a heavy price from indoor air pollution since they spend more time at home breathing in smoke and soot from leaky coal and wood cooking stoves.' Coal is a particularly bad pollutant, hence its contribution as the second largest cause of air pollution-related deaths in the US. Dr Carlos Dora, WHO's Coordinator for Public Health, Environmental and Social Determinants of Health, says: 'Excessive air pollution is often a by-product of unsustainable policies in sectors such as transport, energy, waste management and industry.'[14]

Governments getting sued

What happens when sovereign states sign agreements with the US and then new governments resist American efforts to take over their national resources, including roads and cars?

The Washington-based International Centre for Settlement of Investment Disputes was founded through the UN's World

Bank in 1965 as a court of arbitration for states and corporations. There are currently 3,000 international investment agreements and investor-State dispute settlement clauses (ISDSs) are present in most of them. ISDSs are unique instruments which, in contrast to human rights law and international environmental laws, allow companies and citizens to sue host governments for alleged violations of investment agreements.

ISDSs amount to protection for US businesses, as the Office of the US Trade Representative explains. Agreement to ISDS is 'assurance' by governments to corporations 'that the property of investors will not be seized by the government without the payment of just compensation'. Notice that the onus is not on corporations assuring governments that national assets will not be privatized, their workforces exploited, or their environments harmed. The Office of the Trade Representative says explicitly: 'Military interventions in the early years of US history – gunboat diplomacy – were often in defense of private American commercial interests.' ISDSs are today's gunboats.[15]

The US is party to just 50 of the 3,000 international agreements. 'Governments put ISDS in place... [t]o signal potential investors that the rule of law will be respected', the Office of the Trade Representative continues. 'Rule of law' in this sense essentially means the ability of corporations to do as they please, within wide limits. 'Because of the safeguards in US agreements and because of the high standards of our legal system,' the Office continues, 'foreign investors rarely pursue arbitration against the United States and have never been successful when they have done so... we have never once lost an ISDS case.' Not only this, but 'in a number of instances, panels have awarded the United States attorneys fees after the United States successfully defended frivolous or otherwise non-meritorious claims'. The Office further notes the protection afforded US corporations at the expense of host governments: 'The United States has put in place several layers of defenses to minimize the risk that US agreements could be exploited in the manner to which other agreements among other countries are susceptible.'[16]

In addition to understanding how ISDS clauses amount to protection for US corporations, it is also worth noting that many ISDS cases appear to involve energy and energy-service issues.

According to the UN's Conference on Trade and Development (UNCTAD), out of the 3,000 global trade and investment arrangements, 608 (data from the year 2014) resulted in an ISDS dispute, of which 356 cases are now concluded. The high number of ongoing cases suggests that corporations like to drain states' resources by dragging out disputes. EU Member States (minus the smaller countries) are the main users of the ISDS clause, accounting for over 50 per cent of cases. 'EU Member States have rarely been challenged by investors from outside the EU', says the European Commission (EC). However, bilateral deals may change that. The EC reports that the most frequently used instruments involve the Energy Charter (60 cases), NAFTA (53) and the Argentina-US Bilateral Investment Treaty (17), which, as the Office of the US Trade Representative indicates, means that the majority of cases brought against the US will result in defeat for the plaintiff.[17]

There is no apparent legal obligation to make the details of ISDSs public. It is therefore difficult to obtain facts and figures on the number of cases that have been brought forward. 'In many instances, disputes remain confidential. It is therefore difficult to make a complete assessment', says the EC. By the end of 2014, including the 356 determined cases, only 37 per cent were awarded in favour of the state; 28 per cent were settled (which could amount to the state compromising for the investor); and 25 per cent were found in favour of investors. Eight per cent were discontinued. According to the EC, in 30 per cent of cases, no public information is available. Eight per cent of known cases involved transnational corporations. This comparatively small percentage is either due to corporations having so much influence over governments that they need to threaten governments in courts only occasionally, or that many cases have been brought against governments in secret.[18]

According to UNCTAD, the majority of ISDS cases concern individuals or corporations challenging governments over alleged violations of contracts, concessions, cancellations, revocations and/or denials of permits and licences. UNCTAD reckons that between 61 and 70 per cent of new cases

(2013/14 data) involve claims in the services sector, including banking, energy (gas and electricity), media, real estate and telecommunications.[19]

Reporting to a House of Lords committee on TTIP, Dr Lauge Poulsen of Oxford University suggested that under a Free Trade Agreement (FTA), Britain 'should expect to be subject to at least as many claims as were filed by US investors against Canada under the NAFTA agreement'. This is largely due to the similar percentage of foreign direct investment that the US enjoys in the UK and Canada. Although TTIP appears to be dead, this could be bad news for the UK as its leaders are intent on signing post-Brexit 'free trade' deals.[20] Let us examine some specific cases of governments sued by corporations under ISDS.

Under the title, 'Canada is the most sued country in the "developed" world', globalization specialist Maude Barlow writes that in 35 ISDS cases against Canada, the government forked out $153 million to US corporations. Another $194 billion is being sought and $51 million has already been spent by the government defending itself. Two-thirds of the cases involve environmental protection and resource management.[21]

Under Chapter 11 of NAFTA, the Delaware-based oil and gas company Lone Pine Resources Inc is suing the Canadian government for at least $118.9 million under the arbitration rules of the UN Commission on International Trade Law (UNCITRAL). Lone Pine's Canadian subsidiary LPRC states that it has five exploration licences for petroleum, gas and underground reservoirs near the town of Trois-Rivières. The licences originated with the Canadian company Junex Inc. In 2011, a Quebec law (*An Act to Limit Oil and Gas Activities*) came into force and LPRC's exploration licence for the St Lawrence River was revoked. LPRC's claim is that the original Junex licences entitle the company to explore in the River. LPRC also claims that the revocation of the licence has been conducted without compensation to the company and alleges that, 'this measure violates the legitimate expectations that it had when it decided to invest in Quebec', says the government of Canada. Their position is that LPRC does not possess export licences, but rather, that the licences are owned by Junex.

The government also says that Article 1105 of NAFTA is not a protection of investors' expectations. Finally, the Canadian government claims that 'passing the Act is a legitimate exercise of the Government of Quebec's police power and, thus, the measure cannot constitute an expropriation'.[22]

The case is a blow to environmental activists and legislators; even if Canada wins, it demonstrates the tenacity of corporations.

Another US vs Canada case involves the compound known as MTT, a fuel additive that enhances the octane value of unleaded petrol. The Canadian government maintained that its proposed MTT Act was in place to prohibit interprovincial trading for environmental reasons. The Ethyl Corporation, based in Virginia and operating through its Canadian subsidiary, was the sole importer and interprovincial MTT trader. Under Chapter 11 of NAFTA, the corporation was supposed to receive 'national treatment' in Canada and took the Canadian government to court for violating its obligations, claiming that the government was raising environmental concerns merely as a protective mechanism to favour Canadian corporations. Canada challenged the jurisdiction of the International Convention on the Settlement of Investment Disputes – the tribunal to which bilateral FTA cases may be brought – pointing out that the Ethyl Corporation had failed to give due notice and that the MTT Act had not yet received Royal Assent. The outcome was that Canada lost its appeal and had to pay the Ethyl Corporation and the court costs.[23]

Turning the situation around, let's look at a case of the US raising barriers against Canada under the guise of environmental concerns.

The Vancouver-based Methanex corporation (and subsidiaries) manufactured a feedstock for the fuel additive MTBE. California ruled that MTBE contaminated drinking water and introduced an import ban. Methanex called California's move a 'sham environmental protection in order to cater to local political interests or in order to protect a domestic industry'. The corporation alleged that California's then governor, Greg Davis, introduced the prohibition in exchange for campaign contributions from the US agribusiness company Archer Daniel Midlands. The Tribunal ruled in California's favour.[24]

Examining cases outside Canada, the litigation follows a similar pattern. Manuel Pérez-Rocha at the US Institute for Policy Studies writes that 'countries from Indonesia to Peru are facing investor-state suits. Mexico and Canada have lost or settled five each under NAFTA, paying hundreds of millions of dollars to foreign companies'. In 2012, Ecuador was ordered to pay just under $1.77 billion to a subsidiary of the Texas-based Occidental Petroleum for contract cancellations. The case was annulled and Ecuador settled to pay just over $900 million. Venezuela was ordered to pay $1.6 billion to the Texas-based Exxon to compensate for oil nationalization. 'Nearly 200 disputes are pending', writes Pérez-Rocha. According to UNCTAD, 75 per cent of claims are brought by US and European businesses.[25]

Sweden's power company Vattenfall sued Germany over its decision to phase out nuclear energy. A single energy policy change resulted in seven ISDS claims being brought against the Czech Republic and six in Spain. Citing a 1999 investment law, Pacific Rim sued the government of El Salvador in 2009, following a moratorium on gold mining introduced by the country in the preceding year. 'For El Salvador, a $301 million loss – just under two per cent of its GDP – would significantly reduce funds available for healthcare and education.'[26]

Whether a corporation is wrong or right to sue a government is beside the point. The most important issue is that the taxpayer pays, meaning that budgets allocated to health and education are jeopardized. ISDSs amount to indirect attacks on socialist-orientated government policies. What happened in Ecuador is a particularly instructive case.

Ecuadorian President Sixto Durán-Ballén (1992-96) led the country's accession to the WTO and privatized state assets. In 1993, Ecuador signed the Encouragement and Reciprocal Protection of Investments bilateral investment treaty (BIT) with the US. In 1999, within the framework of the BIT, PetroEcuador agreed a deal with the Texas-based Occidental Exploration and Production Company (OEPC), a subsidiary of Occidental Petroleum. The companies agreed to explore for hydrocarbons in Bloc 15 of the Ecuadorian Amazon, covering about 200,000 hectares. The Participation Contract involved OEPC sharing oil revenues in exchange for exploring and extracting. The Participation Contract states that the deal was to be 'governed exclusively by Ecuadorian law'.[27]

OEPC wanted to farm out work on Bloc 15 and did so by attempting to sell 40 per cent of its equity stake in Bloc 15 to a Bermuda-based financial company, City Investing Company Limited, whose mother company was Alberta Energy Corporation. Under Ecuadorian law, the deal was not permitted. In 2001, Ecuador's tax authority changed the practice of refunding value added taxes to oil companies, retrospectively claiming refunds of VAT. OEPC sought arbitration against Ecuador for a so-called VAT Award. The VAT Tribunal awarded $75 million to OEPC. The British High Court rejected Ecuador's appeal.[28]

In 2006, the government of Ecuador issued the *Caducidad* Decree to OEPC, terminating the Participation Contract, ordering OEPC to turn its assets over to PetroEcuador. Also in that year, Ecuador passed Law 42, determining that 50 per cent of windfall revenues belong to the state. In 2012, the Tribunal issued an award to OEPC, stating that the government has acted in ways 'tantamount to expropriation' and in violation of treaty obligations to treat OEPC as favourably as a national corporation. The Tribunal ordered Ecuador to pay $1.7 billion of taxpayers' money to OEPC. OEPC agreed to settle for a smaller pay-out of $980 million but the cost to Ecuadorian taxpayers was still disastrous – just before this the government had announced an $800-million cut in social spending resulting from the contraction of the country's oil revenues.[29]

8 Food and agriculture: 'Mere law'

How poor standards in US food and biotech industries could be exported to Europe and post-Brexit Britain via trade deals.

According to the World Food Programme, '795 million people in the world do not have enough food to lead a healthy active life'. Food is a commodity, not a basic right. The industry is worth $4 trillion annually and, with banks and hedge funds speculating on the rise and fall of the price of corn, meat, wheat and other staples, prices are artificially pushed higher than many can afford.[1]

The starving include many of the 24,000 children who die daily from lack of access to food, clean water, medicine and healthcare. The food-insecure total includes the four million Britons who regularly go 24 hours without food in the wake of Conservative-imposed austerity. The biggest food producers in the world by country are China, India and the US, with US mechanization meaning that just two million or so people are employed in agriculture compared with China, where 310 million individuals are employed – a workforce almost the size of the US population. Mechanization has meant consolidation in the agriculture, biotech and chemical industries, as well as worker insecurity, which is great for profits.[2]

Free trade: 'correcting imbalances'

Over the centuries, countries have stopped producing for domestic and local consumption and have increasingly produced for export, even countries with comparatively high rates of malnutrition and starvation like Brazil, China and India. Agriculture and agribusiness-related industries are worth about $830 billion per annum to the US, or 4.8 per cent of US GDP. Farm output accounts for $177 billion or one per cent of GDP, while agricultural exports amount to over $130 billion per annum. The two million farmers in the US farm 373 million hectares. Measured in millions of tonnes (mt) per year, the US produces corn (350mt), cow's milk (91mt), soybeans (89mt), wheat (58mt), potatoes (20mt), chicken (17mt), tomatoes (12mt), beef (11.7mt) and pig meat (10mt). Most of the produce is either genetically modified or affected by genetically modified organisms (GMOs).[3]

In terms of revenue, the US is the biggest seed market, followed by Europe and the Asia-Pacific region. The US 'drives' the market in North America, while China and India 'drive the Asia-Pacific market', says MarketsandMarkets, a website offering 'emerging opportunities' analysis. France and Germany are the leading European players, with Brazil leading Latin America. The global seed market consists of four elements: oilseed (canola/rape, cotton, soybean, sunflower), grain (corn, millet, rice, wheat), fruit and vegetables and miscellaneous products (alfalfa, clover and forage, flower seeds and turf). Of these, grain captures the biggest market share, with rice being the main staple worldwide. The US-EU seed sector controls $20 billion of the global market, which by 2012 was worth $44 billion, a figure that market analysts projected would nearly double by 2018. Rising food demand is another factor. The MarketsandMarkets analysis envisions a big future for GMOs: 'Biotech seeds are consequently seen as those products which can improve the return on investment'.[4]

Agribusiness has a big and powerful lobby in the US. The farm and insurance industries spent over $50 million in the 2012 election cycle lobbying Congress. In total, the federal government spends $20 billion a year on subsidies, overwhelmingly to large companies. The government's $40,000-per-farm subsidy cap is overcome by insurance on which the US Department of Agriculture (USDA) spends about $14 billion per annum to protect farmers against losses, an amount that, Congress reports, has grown sevenfold since 2000. The federal government contracts 18 insurance companies to allow farmers to buy coverage. This means that under a TTIP-style bilateral arrangement, Europe, including the UK, will try to compete with subsidized US agribusiness.[5]

After Brazil, the US is Europe's second-largest supplier of agricultural products. Since 1999, US agriculture trade with the EU has declined because of protectionist measures raised by Europe and retaliatory measures raised by the US (more below). By 2015, the US was running a $12-billion trade deficit with the EU. The US accounted for 10 per cent of Europe's imports by 2015, compared with 17 per cent in 1995. The decline in US exports to the EU is attributed by the USDA to dollar appreciation, commodity prices and 'market access restrictions on a number of our most competitive commodities'. Over the past two decades, EU agricultural exports to the US have doubled. Unlike other sectors with low tariffs, tariff and non-tariff import requirements on agriculture are an impediment to US exports.[6]

It is not surprising, then, that agribusiness led the TTIP lobbying crusade.

US agricultural exports to the EU are nuanced. While bulk commodities have declined by 30 per cent, consumer-orientated goods have grown by over 50 per cent, as a result of European consumer demand. These include (in millions of US dollars per annum), distilled spirits ($770m), wine and beer ($685m), processed fruit ($328m), beef ($306m), processed vegetables ($171m), fruit and vegetable juices ($129m), fresh vegetables ($103m) and tree nuts ($2.9m). Soybean exports remained stable, despite declining commodity prices.[7]

The EU has preferential trade agreements with over 50 countries, including Chile, Colombia, Mexico, Peru and South Africa. Agricultural shipments from these countries (and others) have doubled since 1990, as imports from the US have declined. 'Tariff preferences granted to these countries give them an advantage over US exports', says the USDA. The Central American-Dominican Republic Free Trade Agreement (CAFTA-DR) with the EU gives countries in the region 'an advantage over US exports'. The principal foods exported by CAFTA-DR countries to the EU include tropical fruits and spirits. 'The US-EU TTIP negotiations provide an opportunity for the United States to correct these imbalances', said the USDA before Trump decided to stall or kill TTIP. Of serious concern for consumers, the USDA report says that reducing 'regulatory barriers, in particular unjustified health-and-safety measures, could provide new access for US exports'.[8]

The Corporate Europe Observatory says that, by 2014, there had been 560 meetings between policymakers and corporate representatives on the issue of TTIP. The private sector accounted for 92 per cent of the lobbyists and consultants, with only 4 per cent coming from the public-interest sector; the remaining were academics and individuals. This is a ratio of 20:1 in favour of corporations against trade unions and consumer groups. In many cases, the EU's trade commission department actively sought to include corporations and their representatives in talks, such as pesticide lobbying group the European Crop Protection Association. One email between representatives written in October 2012 refers to 'the European crop protection/pesticides industry' as being 'one of the key sectors we would be looking at in terms of improving the framework for business'.[9]

The Corporate Europe Observatory published leaked emails from 2014 between US and EU seed trade associations. One redacted email from an EU minister discusses their invitation by the US Trade Representative to a meeting with the American Seed Trade Association and the European Seed Association, which have collaborated on a joint TTIP paper. The organizations are focusing on 'priority issues', namely phytosanitary issues (plant health), breeding techniques, and 'the presence of GMOs in conventional seed'.[10]

Food: 'improving market access'

The leaked TTIP and TISA drafts and, more crucially, the economic powers behind them, indicate the character of future bilateral FTAs between the US and European countries, including the UK.

The leaked TTIP draft chapter, 'Agriculture [US: Market Access] Consolidated Proposals', claims to safeguard 'public health, safety, environment [and] public morals'. It goes on to talk about taking measures on 'cultural diversity that each side deems appropriate'. So, if a huge lobby at the European Commission level is able to pressure technocrats to issue directives conducive to corporate welfare, the public safety net is compromised. On the other hand, European environmental protection, such as the labelling provisions on genetically modified foods, may be invoked against the TTIP. Under TTIP or a future bilateral deal, this could result in European member states facing arbitration. With Britain outside the EU, protections against US agriculture may be weakened. The same article states: 'Both Parties will seek to ensure that the effect of such measures does not create unnecessary obstacles to trade in agricultural goods.'[11]

One Article states that the signatory 'substantially improves market access for agricultural goods' and 'develops disciplines that eliminate restrictions on a person's [specifically, a corporate person's] right to export agricultural goods; and... substantially reduces trade-distorting domestic support', such as subsidies to business. As noted, the US already subsidizes agribusiness. Another Article suggests that TTIP will set a standard that forces non-members to comply via tariff reductions. It states: 'The Parties shall not grant any financial support to exports of an agricultural good... where the non-Party has fully eliminated duties on that agricultural good for the benefit of both Parties.'[12]

So non-TTIP members could pay higher prices than TTIP members.

Like TTIP, the chapter of the Trans-Pacific Partnership (TPP) on agriculture is far-reaching. We can use the TPP example (which applies mainly to Asian countries) to see what might happen under new 'free trade' deals.

One TPP Article includes as biotechnology 'fish and fish products, developed using modern biotechnology, but does not include medicines and medical products'. Another cites 'the elimination of trade distorting restrictions on the authorization to export agricultural goods'. This threatens health-and-safety standards because, even though TPP legislation states that signatories are not obliged to change domestic laws with respect to consumer rights and environmental protection, acting on existing legislation (such as restrictions on hormone-treated beef), could be cited by the US government as interference in their profit-making.[13]

Citing General Agreement on Tariffs and Trade rules, another TPP Article states that 'a Party may temporarily apply an export prohibition or restriction... to prevent or relieve a critical shortage of foodstuffs'. So, assuming President Trump goes ahead with similar bilateral deals, if US biotech companies start operating in Vietnam, as they have in the Philippines, using cheap Vietnamese labour and lacklustre testing standards, they can expect GM crops to be re-exported for use across Asia – and even the US and Europe. However, if Vietnam suffers a flood and a crop is wiped out, it may choose to use food grown for export – foreign or domestic, GMO or otherwise – to feed its people. In theory, the TPP Article protects this right but in reality countries have already been challenged (as India was challenged by the US at the WTO) for saving food for hungry populations. Again, this serves as an example of the kind of things that might happen if our governments sign more 'free trade' deals.[14]

In November 2014, the US and India worked out a deal on a thorny issue which hitherto had prevented a trade agreement. The US had introduced the Trade Facilitation Agreement and India had refused to endorse it. India and other poor countries stated that food stockpiling is a necessary insurance against poor harvests and food-price fluctuations in the market. 'But stockpiling and subsidies for the poor are considered trade-distort[ions] under existing WTO rules,' writes Agence France-Presse. In the 19th century, the British colonial authority deliberately withheld grain and rice from starving Indians, who, due to seed-saving techniques, had rarely experienced famine prior to the British conquest. This had the intended effect (as historian and sociologist Mike Davis documents extensively) of artificially inflating prices on the London Stock Exchange and benefiting speculators. Today, food shortages also help keep the market afloat. Never mind that 400 million Indians at any one time are severely malnourished. Agence France-Presse concludes: 'Western countries, led by the United States, have raised concerns that [food] stocks could leak onto global markets, skewing trade'.[15]

In 2014, the American Seed Trade Association and the European Seed Association issued a joint statement, claiming that 'requests of "100-per-cent purity" or "absolute zero tolerances"' with regard to plant safety and biotech 'are terms that are compatible with neither the realities of plant breeding, seed production, agriculture in open-field environments nor with the practicalities of increasing international trade in seed and commodities'.[16]

The 'Sanitary and Phytosanitary Measures' contained in TTIP seek to ensure 'that the Parties' sanitary and phytosanitary (SPS) measures do not create unnecessary barriers to trade'. The Chapter also states that health-and-safety standards should ultimately lie with domestic legislation. In countries with lax environmental and health-and-safety standards, TTIP-inspired bilateral deals will boost profits for biotech companies. 'The final determination whether a sanitary measure maintained by an exporting Party achieves the importing Party's appropriate level of sanitary protection rests solely with the importing Party acting in accordance with its administrative and legislative framework', says another Article.[17]

The wording of the draft text is ambiguous enough to allow for arbitration. It could be taken to mean that the US, wanting to export a certain product to make a certain drug, has to fund its own safety checks to meet EU requirements. On the other hand, it could mean that the EU is abandoning its health-and-safety obligations for imports and is, instead, relying on the US to police itself. The wording is vague enough to be challenged through an ISDS. Another Article, 'Information Exchange', is a measure to protect corporations from public disclosure. It is not a provision to safeguard public health.[18] We need to watch out for this kind of provision in bilateral 'free trade' deals as well.

Pesticides: 'no official safe limit'

The European Commission states: 'So-called "niche" crops are ones like parsley, leeks, celery or lettuce, where at the moment the market isn't as big as for other crops like wheat or maize (corn)' – which are now 80 per cent genetically modified. 'We want to help farmers produce more of these niche crops. To do that they need to be able to use certain pesticides, at levels which studies have proved are safe', the report continues. 'In many cases no-one has yet carried out these studies. So there's no official safe limit, and farmers can't use the pesticides in question for these crops.'[19]

Pesticides include deterrents, growth regulators, repellents and toxins. Traditional organic pesticides include Chinese lemon eucalyptus and Indian citronella, which repel mosquitoes; cedar, geraniol, pine oils and thyme, which repel malaria vectors; and the pyrethrum daisy of Persia to prevent insect attacks on flowers.[20]

Over the centuries, the growth of a state-subsidized chemical industry, with its ties to the military, has resulted in the widespread use of synthetic pesticides. Nerve-gas weapons utilize organophosphorus compounds – the same as pesticides – which affect humans by disrupting the electrochemistry of nerve cells. The agent VX, for example, stockpiled by the US as a chemical weapon, can kill a human in less than 10 minutes. It was developed into a commercial pesticide, Amiton, and sold on the British market. Today, Monsanto's Roundup, a glyphosate banned by the EU until recently, is used by the US government, contracting DynCorp, to spray and kill biodiversity in Colombia under the pretext of a war on drugs.[21]

Each year, pesticide poisoning kills 20,000 people and poisons a further three million. Of these deaths, 99 per cent occur in poor countries, such as Ghana and India, despite the fact that poor countries use lower quantities of pesticides as compared with the industrialized West. Lack of education about the dangers, the use of child labour in agriculture, and poor health-and-safety standards in general are cited as key factors. The use of illegal pesticides is another factor, with a third of those used in India falling below government standards. Across Asia and the Pacific, 82 of the most commonly used pesticides (including 7 out of the 10 most commonly used) are moderately to highly toxic. In Indonesia, 44 per cent of the pesticides used fall under the WHO's classification 'moderately to extremely hazardous'.[22]

The pesticide industry is worth $31 billion. The big five

producers are DuPont, Syngenta, Dow, BASF and Bayer (which recently bought the sixth giant, Monsanto). Each year, Europe uses 200,000 tonnes of pesticide. Proposed health-and-safety legislation is seen as an impediment to the US chemical industry. Lobbyists have successfully removed some EU legislation against pesticides.[23]

In 2012, the American Chemistry Council (ACC) and CropLife America (CLA) wrote a letter of concern to the US Office of Chemical Safety and Pollution Prevention. They noted that ACC and CLA are aware of 'a potential US-EU Free Trade Agreement' and that they 'have been monitoring plans of the European Commission... to regulate pesticide and other chemicals which may exert adverse effects through endocrine pathways'. It continues: 'ACC and CLA have serious concerns that the Commission's proposed regulatory categorization process would trigger negative and far-reaching impacts on global commerce.' The letter notes: 'The business of chemistry is a $760-billion enterprise and a key element of the nation's economy. It is the largest exporting sector in the US.'[24]

Certain chemicals present in everyday products, from plastics to pesticides, are endocrine disruptors. It is only recently that health organizations have begun to take seriously the risks associated with endocrine-disrupting chemicals (EDCs). The chemicals are linked to cancer and infertility and have cost public-health services €157 billion ($183.6 bn). When EDCs are identified above a certain quantity in products, the products are banned under the EU's REACH regulations 2006, pesticide regulations (1107/2009) and biocide regulations (528/2012). With a huge chemical industry, European regulations constraining the importation and commercialization of products containing EDCs are a threat to US and European corporate profit maximization.[25]

Due to controversy over the definition, the Directorate-General for the Environment of the European Commission was tasked with establishing definitive scientific criteria. European chemical giants Bayer and BASF were also keen to lobby against health and safety. The WHO/International Programme on Chemical Safety defines EDCs as follows: 'an exogenous substance or mixture that alters function(s) of the endocrine system and consequently causes adverse health effects in an intact organism, or its progeny, or (sub)populations'. This definition lent support to the EU-commissioned Kortenkamp Report of 2012. Even prior to the report, Germany and the UK worked against the EU criteria, citing the 'commercial impact' of health-and-safety regulation on business and reserving the ban for the most toxic potencies. The threshold idea was developed by the European Centre for Ecotoxicology and Toxicology of Chemicals, whose sponsors include BASF, Bayer, Dow and Syngenta.[26]

Deregulation was promoted in Brussels by Conservative MEP Julie Girling, who established the Informal Working Group on Risk-based Policy Making. Girling invited Anne Glover, Chief Scientific Adviser to the President of the EU Commission, to talk at an event attended by chemical lobbyists CEFIC, ECPA, PlasticsEurope, the Toy Industries of Europe and delegates from BASF, Bayer, ECETOC and ExxonMobil (oil being a basic product for the plastic and pesticides industry). The talk was in response to Swedish socialist MEP Åsa Westlund's report on the dangers of endocrine-disrupting chemicals. A WHO/UNEP report from 2013 refers to EDCs as a 'global threat that needs to be resolved'. In spring 2013, Europe's Directorate-Generals had rejected their colleague's proposals for tighter legislation on EDCs. The UK's assessment was alarmist, stating that regulations on pesticides would cause a 20-per-cent loss in annual wheat, potato and oilseed rape yields. European Commission Secretary-General Catherine Day authorized the publication of an impact assessment on EDCs, which the lobbyists had pushed for as a delaying tactic.[27]

CropLife specifically referred to TTIP in its correspondence with EC commissioners, voicing concern that EDC regulation is not in the spirit of the TTIP negotiations. At present, negotiations have stalled – hence Trump's bilateral approach to trade deals.[28]

GMOs: believing in choice

Genetically Modified Organisms (GMOs) are everywhere. Globally, there are approximately 160 million hectares of genetically modified crops. These include alfalfa, beet, canola, corn, cotton, maize, papaya, potato, squash and sugar beet.* Under Trump's trade deals, American GMO companies will find it easier to push their products on the European market. Barriers may be seen as market interference by corporations. Investor-State dispute settlements, which are costly to taxpayers, and retaliatory measures, which are costly to consumers, may result from governments reacting to public pressure to ban or limit GMOs.[29]

The EU has passed legislation demanding that foods containing GMOs at least be labelled. After Brexit, Britain will be more vulnerable to GMO penetration by US firms.

Plant and animal species are genetically modified (GM) when the DNA from one plant or animal is spliced with another to produce a genetically modified organism. In 1973, Boyer and Cohen created the first GMO: an antibiotic-resistant gene spliced into a plasmid. The first GM animal was produced in 1974 by Rudolf Jaenisch, when a DNA virus was spliced into a mouse embryo. In 1976, Boyer and Swanson formed the first GM company, Genetech, which produced GM insulin. In 1981, it was demonstrated that injecting DNA into a single-cell mouse embryo can lead to intergenerational modification. In 1983, Bevan and his research team produced the first GM plant: an agrobacterium with an antibiotic resistant gene. In 1987, an ice-resistant strain of *P. syringae* was the first GMO to be released in the environment when potato and strawberry fields in California were sprayed with the product. The purpose was to prevent cold-related die-off and increase sales and profits.[30]

In 1992, under Council Directive 90/220/EEC, GM animal feed was approved by the European Union.[31]

In 1994, the Calgene company was authorized to sell the first GM food, the Flavr Savr tomato. In the same year, the EU approved a herbicide-resistant GM tobacco, making it the first GMO on sale in Europe. The Sanitary and Phytosanitary Agreement provides a scientific basis for judging import

---

* By 2004, the US was growing 47.6 million hectares (mh), Argentina 16.2mh, Brazil 5mh, Canada 5.4mh, China 3.7mh and India 0.5mh. Ten years later, the US was growing 73.1mh of GM crops, Argentina 24.3mh, Brazil 42.2mh, India and Canada 11.6mh and China 3.9mh.

restrictions based on health-and-safety considerations. It was enacted at the GATT Uruguay Round in 1995, and the WTO was authorized to administer the details. The rule is supposed to balance the sovereignty requirements of signatory member states with the wishes of corporations that their imports/ exports are not 'arbitrarily' disrupted.[32]

In 1999, under the name Genetic Use Restriction Technology (aka 'suicide seeds' or 'terminator technology'), the US Department of Agriculture and the Delta and Pine Land Company announced the development of GM seeds that would become infertile after a growing season. The aim was supposedly to prevent piracy by making farmers pay to use the crop. However, the actual effect is to make farmers unable to grow or save seed, rendering growers reliant on Monsanto (now part of Bayer), which acquired the technology. The company claims that it has never commercialized the technology due to immense opposition. Haley Stein in the *Northwestern Journal of Technology and Intellectual Property*, states: 'One of the major frustrations for the private seed industry is the perseverance of the seed-saving tradition among farmers.' Writing in the oxymoronically titled *Journal of Business Ethics*, Keith Bustos notes: 'It seems as though the [anti-terminator technology] activists take a right to save seed derived from one's crop to be a *prima facie* right.'[33]

Also in 1999, it was reported that Britain's Parliamentary catering committee, led by Dennis Turner MP, banned GM foods from government canteens. At the same time, Prime Minster Tony Blair was advising the public to give GMOs a try. In the same year, Monsanto confirmed to Friends of the Earth that it had removed all GM products from its own cafeteria at a pharmaceutical factory in Buckinghamshire because it 'believes in choice' (Monsanto spokesperson Tony Coombes). The industry doesn't seem to believe in choice for consumers, when it sells GM feedstock to farmers, who then sell meat products to the public without notifying them that the animals have been fed with modified organisms.[34]

By that year, the GM industry was worth $2.3 billion, with 40 million hectares (around 100 million acres) of GM crops grown worldwide. The industry has contracted lately, with the growth of the organic food market and consumer preference for non-GMOs. This has forced the GMO industry to disguise its products by selling mainly to farmers, who use GM feedstock. In 1999, the US Public Broadcasting Service (PBS) reported that, in addition to GMOs in animal feed, processed foods 'contain varying amounts of GM ingredients', because companies use different GM ingredients at different points in the production cycle. The contraction of the industry was partly due to EU labelling laws.[35]

'Regulation (EC) No 1829/2003 of the European Parliament and of the Council of 22 September 2003 on genetically modified food and feed' states that GMOs must be subject to a 'safety assessment' (Article 3) prior to commercialization. As no authorization procedure existed for approving GMOs in animal feed, Article 11 states that such procedures should be introduced. Article 17 reaffirms 'the right of consumers to information' and specifically states the necessity of labelling so that 'the consumer [can] make an informed choice'.[36]

By 2013, most British supermarkets had lifted their self-imposed restrictions on selling GMOs because, as PBS had already noted in the 1990s, there is so much GM material in processed food and animal feedstock that supermarkets found it economically 'unviable' to maintain the prohibition. A farm conference recently revealed that 80 per cent of animal feedstock (maize and soya beans) is GM. 'We find it convenient not to make a big noise about it,' says Professor David Hughes of Imperial College London. Conor McVeigh, representing McDonald's, revealed that the company sells beef products from cows fed with GMOs, noting: '[it is] becoming increasingly difficult to source non-GM feed within our supply chain.' Peter Melchett of the Soil Association UK advised that British livestock be fed domestic products, instead of GM crops grown in the US and Brazil.[37]

The British Conservative government is keen to push GMOs, advising in Parliamentary committees that domestic disclosure laws and regulations with regard to field trials should be amended to give corporations, scientists, research councils and other involved parties greater anonymity. Following the successful destruction of GM crop trials by direct activists, the British government is 'seeking to facilitate the hosting of GM trials at suitable sites that can provide greater security if required... and will continue to work with the police to ensure that... property is protected'. The committee concludes: 'We recommend that the Government consider amending the Genetically Modified Organisms (Deliberate Release) Regulations 2002 to remove the requirement that researchers publicly disclose the six-figure grid reference location of planned field trials, in order to assist GM crop field trials and reduce the burden of security costs.'[38]

Golden Rice is a Monsanto sideline that was sponsored by the Bill and Melinda Gates Foundation. It is biosynthesized beta-carotene designed to boost vitamin A, a deficiency in which kills an estimated 700,000 children a year. In 2013, the UK's Environment Secretary, Owen Paterson, described people who oppose GMOs as 'absolutely wicked'. Paterson justified his sentiments as follows: 'It's just disgusting that little children are allowed to go blind and die because of a hang-up by a small number of people about this technology.' Paterson had nothing to say about the 'virtuous' corporations speculating on food prices, the 'righteous' legislators at the World Trade Organization who deem seed storage a threat to markets, or the 'moral' architects of the globalized economy, which shifts food production from localized subsistence to exports.[39]

What's in your meat?

The four big US meat producers are Cargill Meat Solutions, JBS, National Beef Packing and Tyson Foods. Fast-food chains are big meat purchasers, with McDonald's coming top. Each year in the US, 9 billion broiler chickens, 250 million turkeys, 113 million pigs and 33 million cows are slaughtered. Annually, the US government subsidizes the dairy, egg, fish and meat industries to the tune of $38 billion. Subsidies supposedly help keep prices low for consumers. The figure is higher than the official subsidy because feed grain subsidies are included: over 10 years, corn producers received $84 billion from the government and soybean growers $27 billion, often making it cheaper to buy the products than to grow them.[40]

Dr Neal Barnard of George Washington University estimated that if cancer, diabetes, heart disease and other meat-related illnesses are factored into federal medical costs, there was, by 1992, a $61-billion initial hidden subsidy. Today, lawyer David Robinson Simon reckons external costs which amount to subsidies (including environmental costs) amount to $414 billion. US meat sales were $186 billion in 2011 – 'more than the GDP of Hungary or Ukraine', says Marta Zaraska of *Salon*. Four pork producers control two-thirds of the market. Four beef producers control three-quarters of the market. Tyson Food's annual revenue is $34 billion: 20 times the GDP of Belize. Seed companies which supply feedstock, and drug companies which provide vaccines and antibiotics, are also part of the meat industry, as 60 per cent of the corn and nearly 50 per cent of the soybeans grown annually in the US are used for animal feed.[41]

One particular type of meat subsidy means that beef producers pay $1 per bovine head per $100 value. Over two decades, these were worth $1.2 billion. The industry explains that this 'increas[es] domestic and/or international demand'. Much of the revenue goes back into advertising and accounts for some 11.3 per cent of consumption, according to industry estimates.[42]

Of the US meat industry's massive turnover, only $165 million derives from sales to the EU, which imposes its quality criteria on most beef products. The US meat industry is, in general, targeting the EU to boost exports. TTIP, or its replacements, might be a golden opportunity for the US meat industry to circumvent EU rules governing the ban on importing meat products treated with growth hormones. The British public is particularly vulnerable in the wake of Brexit.

Around 30 animal growth products are available in the US. Farmers started feeding and injecting their cattle with growth hormones in the 1950s. Two-thirds of cattle (including 90 per cent of those on feedlots) are now fed or injected with growth hormones. Growth hormones reduce feedstock costs and produce cows with leaner carcasses, which consumers apparently prefer. The hormones used include estradiol, progesterone and testosterone, as well as synthetic hormones trenbolone acetate and zeranol. Melengestrol acetate is a feedstock additive used to improve weight. Australia, Canada, Chile, Japan, Mexico, New Zealand and South Africa also permit the use of growth hormones.[43]

In 1989, the EU banned US beef treated with growth promoters. By 2003, the EU permanently banned estradiol-17B and continued to provisionally ban five others. In retaliation, the US erected 100 per cent *ad valorem* duties on certain EU foods, which remained in effect until 1996; in 1999 a second tariff was imposed. Affected products included beef and pork, carrots, chicory, Dijon mustard, goose pâté, Roquefort cheese, truffles and agricultural by-products such as glue and wool grease. Affected countries included Austria, Belgium, Denmark, Finland, France, Greece, Ireland, the Netherlands, Portugal, Spain and Sweden. The UK was unaffected because it signalled support for lifting the ban, which may now be much easier to achieve as a result of Brexit.[44]

The WTO has served as an international forum through which appeals, panels and arbitration proceedings have been used to confront the issue. In 1997, the WTO ruled against the EU, citing its supposed WTO obligations under the Sanitary and Phytosanitary Agreement, which requires risk assessments prior to blanket bans. In 2008 it ruled that the US could maintain trade sanctions and allowed the EU to maintain its prohibition. A few months later (in early 2009), the US announced new high tariffs on EU imports and a subsequent US-EU Memorandum of Understanding agreed to phase in these changes. The Memorandum did not save new EU members – Bulgaria, Cyprus, the Czech Republic, Estonia, Hungary, Latvia, Lithuania, Malta, Poland, Romania, Slovakia and Slovenia – from coming under US sanction. Chewing gum, confectionery, cut flowers, fruits and nuts were also added to the list. In the same year, the US advised that Europe should 'simplify' the rules for animal and plant chemical residue inspections.[45]

Despite dispute settlement proceedings at the WTO, the US and EU continue to disagree on scientific and agricultural issues relating to imports and exports. The EU continues to block hormone-treated beef from the US.[46]

By the 1970s, over 80 per cent of US cattle were being

given the diethylstilbestrol (DES) growth hormone. However, cancers in the daughters of women who were given DES to prevent miscarriages were discovered. Growth hormones are not permitted in pig and poultry production. However, the industry circumvents the rules by using hormone-like products called beta-agonists (ractopamine hydrochloride and zilpaterol hydrochloride).[47]

One such rule-bending drug is recombinant bovine growth hormone (rBGH), given to dairy cattle. It is injected into cows to enhance milk production. Some 17.2 per cent of cows in the US are given the hormone by over 40 per cent of large-scale producers. Banned in Australia, Canada, Europe, Japan, New Zealand and the UK, Monsanto's rBGH was approved by the Food and Drug Administration in 1993 under the name Posilac. Monsanto's own studies demonstrated that Posilac risks clinical mastitis for cows, one of the leading causes of painful bovine mortality, while further Monsanto studies noted lameness and skeletal disorders. Concerns for post-Posilac animal welfare have led to higher rates of culling. Cow pregnancy and birth difficulties, digestive disorders and lactation complications have also been documented.[48]

The meat producer JBS complained that Zilmax, marketed by Intervet (a subsidiary of Merck & Co), caused 20 per cent of its cattle to suffer tender-foot during hot weather. Tyson complained that its cattle could not walk after being treated with Zilmax and ceased purchasing the drug. Datasets suggest that cattle sickness rates were higher in 2014, after the drug came on the market. A study published in the same year found that cattle treated with Zilmax combined with trenbolone acetate and estradiol increased cows' lateral lying and pushing. Eli Lilly's subsidiary Elanco produces ractopamine under the brand name Paylean. Meat processers use it to treat pig products as well as living pigs. After reports of sick and dying pigs, Elanco was requested by the FDA to issue a warning label. Purdue University studies found that Paylean causes cardiac problems and stress-related behaviours, particularly when pigs are transported. This increases the risk of the stressed-out pigs being abused by impatient meat workers.[49]

Two of the biggest growth hormone companies are Elanco

(which produces the beta-agonist ractopamine hydrochloride) and Merck & Co (in the form of Intervet which sells zilpaterol hydrochloride).[50] For the sake of animal welfare, if nothing else, new 'free trade' deals should limit not seek to increase the exportation of drug-and hormone-treated animals by big US producers. But animal welfare is not the only consideration.

Many people have heard of the antibiotic crisis in humans, where more and more strains of bacteria are becoming resistant to the drugs. This is due to the overproduction of antibiotics and, in large part, their use in animal feed. The drugs act as growth hormones and pre-emptive medicines, as many animals for slaughter are kept in filthy, cost-reducing conditions. It is cheaper to drug them with antibiotics than to invest in sanitary conditions. In 2014 President Obama signed an Executive Order to strategize reducing dependence on antibiotics that can stimulate bacterial resistance. But this has proven ineffective. The EU ban on antibacterial drugs for farming only extended to certain drugs and their uses in growth hormone replacements. The last thing we need are 'free trade' deals that allow the exportation of more antiobiotic-fed animal products.

Approximately 14 million kilograms of antibiotics are sold to the farming industry by drug companies each year. In the US, antibiotics are fed to cattle, chickens, pigs and turkeys. Bacteria that cause calf pneumonia, pig dysentery and cattle MRSA are now resistant to many antibiotics. Unlike the EU, Denmark imposed a wide-ranging ban on antibiotic feeds in 2000 and avoided a potential surge in livestock disease by improving husbandry and weaning techniques, including giving the animals more space. The Humane Society Institute for Science and Policy refers to the widespread use of antibiotics in the meat industry as 'a crutch for poor management'. Huge profit is more like it.[51]

In 2015, California became the first US state to ban the use of antibiotics to promote growth.[52]

Intellectual property: public health as 'expropriation'

Intellectual property (IP) covers several fields, including artistic, creative and literary works, biotechnology, medicine, trademarks and geographical indication (such as Roquefort cheese and Scotch whisky). IP rights enable corporations to own the building blocks of life: from medicine to whole genes. The Utah-based Myriad Genetics Inc attempted to isolate and patent the BRCA1 and BRCA2 genes, which are breast-cancer indicators. In doing so, the company attempted to block researchers from testing the genes by charging some $4,000 per test. After a long legal battle, the US Supreme Court rejected Myriad's monopoly plea. That has not deterred Myriad from continuing to litigate against cancer researchers.[53]

As the economy relies more and more on hi-tech, including biotech, 'free trade' deals are increasingly concerned with IP.

The patenting of life has its origins in the 1970s. In 1971, Dr Ananda Chakrabarty of General Electric applied to the US Patent and Trademark Office to patent a GMO engineered to consume oil spills. The proposal was rejected on the grounds that living things are not patentable. Chakrabarty and his paymasters appealed to the Court of Customs and Patent Appeals, whose judges voted in their favour. The decision opened the floodgates, allowing anything but a 'complete' human being to be patented: hence the importance of the Myriad case which indicated some constraints on biotech practices. Since then, there has been a race to patent every gene and combination. In 1984, after a patient called John Moore attended the University of California-Los Angeles for skin cancer treatment, the University and Sandoz Pharmaceuticals obtained and patented his spleen cells (making $3 billion from them), without his knowledge or consent. In 1990, the Supreme Court of California ruled that Mr Moore had no rights over his own cells. By 2003, 127,000 patent applications were filed for human genes and sequences.[54]

IP regulation is internationalized via the WTO's Trade-Related Intellectual Property Rights (TRIPS) agreement. However, bilateral agreements could allow TRIPS rules to be circumvented: 'There is no compelling evidence that a single standard or a standard appropriate for developed countries', such as the TRIPS agreement, 'will certainly maximize the innovative abilities of late-industrializing countries', writes Juan He in the *Chinese Journal of International Law*. Juan He concludes that standardization of IP protection mechanisms 'is unreasonable and unrealistic in that it hampers rather than facilitates achievement of an individually appropriate legal balance'. This is especially so in a system designed by those holding power. Through TRIPS, 'a right owner', such as a biotech firm, 'cannot prevent importation of products embodying its IPRs [intellectual property rights] so long as such products have been put legally on any foreign market'. This means that US companies can undermine development by exporting IP-protected products to poor countries.[55]

The UN's Sub-Committee on the Promotion and Protection of Human Rights (2000) states that the TRIPS provision of the WTO 'does not reflect the fundamental nature and indivisibility of all human rights, including the right of everyone to enjoy the benefits of scientific progress and its applications, the right to health, the right to food, and the right to self-determination'. It concludes that 'there are apparent conflicts between the intellectual property rights regime embodied in the TRIPS Agreement, on the one hand, and international human rights law, on the other'. A report by the UN's Office of the High Commissioner for Human Rights states that the pharmaceutical industry focuses on 'profitable' diseases, such as HIV/AIDS and considers TB, malaria and smaller killers 'bad investments'.[56]

The effects of intellectual property on health can be deadly, as the case of post-apartheid South Africa illustrates. With about 18.5 per cent of the country's population being HIV-positive, the government proposed lowering drug prices, only for the Pharmaceutical Manufacturers' Association of South Africa, which is dominated by Western drug companies, to raise formal objections. Professor William W Fisher of the Harvard Law School writes that, fearing 'a domino effect in the developing world', American drug giants, with the support of the Bill Clinton administration, alleged that South Africa's domestic legislation mandating the lowering of drug prices to help people with HIV was a violation of the TRIPS agreement. A representative of the Bristol-Myers Squibb company said: 'Patents are the lifeblood of our industry. Compulsory licensing [where governments cite national emergencies in order to waive licensing fees] expropriate our patent rights.'[57]

In addition, the protection of testing data in bilateral trade agreements amounts to 'a substitute for patent protection, thereby detracting from the public domain products that should be freely available', writes patent expert Professor Carlos Correa.[58]

Former World Bank chief economist and Nobel laureate Professor Joseph Stiglitz writes: that 'Poorly designed intellectual property regimes can reduce access to technology and medicine, lead to a less efficient economy, and may even slow the pace of innovation'. IP is supposed to protect designers, inventors and authors against piracy. So, when an individual or company develops a drug or the component of a drug, IP will protect a foreign country from 'pirating' that drug. Stiglitz argues that IP restricts knowledge and considers the restriction of knowledge to be a market inefficiency.[59]

One study estimates a decline of 5 to 17 per cent in the generation of public knowledge in the genetics sector as a result of IP protection. IP can also result in monopolization and thus distortion and inequality. Monopoly prices result in lower product utilization among consumers, especially poorer consumers who do not have health insurance. Furthermore, the boundaries of what is and isn't legally patentable are blurred, as in the Chakrabarty case. One way to avoid these distortions would be to introduce a set licensing fee, which the US will not consider.[60]

At the time of writing, there are no IP leaks from TISA, TTIP or bilateral deals, but we can take as an example Chapter 18 of the TPP. Article 18.4(c) commits signatories to 'foster competition and open and efficient markets'. Another Article states that while each party has the national right to determine an 'emergency', under which leasing rights can be waived, it emphasizes 'public health crises', indicating that anything less than a pandemic does not justify a government's use of a patented product without licensing authorization. A further Article commits members to providing 'technical assistance for developing countries'. Poor countries are thus likely to continue depending on the innovations of richer countries without actually being free to chart an independent course. If the Philippines, for instance, allows a US drug company to open a laboratory, under the rules governing foreign direct investment the results could be patented and protected in the US. The drug could then be sold to poorer countries under an expensive IP licensing agreement, having benefited from less expensive Philippine labour and weaker health-and-safety regulations.[61]

Article 18.6.1 'recognize[s]... traditional knowledge' of plants and genes, but includes no safeguards for that knowledge. In fact, a subsection of that Article talks about 'enhanc[ing] the understanding of issues connected with traditional knowledge associated with genetic resources', indicating that the treaty might lock governments and corporations into a knowledge-sharing system where domestic knowledge is taken, patented and licensed by big corporations – in other words, nothing less than piracy by the rich. In an extraordinary statement, another Article claims that patent licences may be excluded in order to protect human, animal and plant health, as well as public morality, 'provided that such exclusion is not made merely because the exploitation is prohibited by its law'.

The South Africa case mentioned above demonstrates how seriously US corporate lawyers take compulsory licensing as a matter of national health.[62]

Part III

Finance and healthcare

9 Financialization: 'A highway without speed limits'

How financial and insurance firms continue to push for deregulation. The bilateral deals favoured by Donald Trump are likely to be as bad as, or worse than, the proposed multilateral deals such as TTIP and TISA.

Long before the Brexit referendum result, Anglo-American investors were discussing a possible US-British Free Trade Agreement (as if ordinary people 'agree' to such things). But what would such an 'agreement' look like? This chapter reminds us what happens when governments deregulate financial institutions.

'Complete dependence on US banks'

Following the worst financial crisis since the Great Depression, President Obama enacted some meagre and weak legislation – the Dodd-Frank Act of 2010 – to curb the reckless behaviour of financial institutions. Lawyers and lobbyists working for big fincance were not happy about Dodd-Frank and pressed hard to repeal it. They were also not happy with the similar regulations imposed by the European Union.[1]

US corporate lawyers struggled to get clear and unequivocal financial deregulation into the Obama-era TTIP drafts. Today, Trump's advisers recommend doing it through bilateral legislation. In 2016, two Trump advisers, Peter Navarro of the University of California-Irvine and billionaire investor Wilbur Ross, published a trade agenda. 'Excessive regulation drives up costs, drives down both R&D and hiring, and contributes to the "push" offshore of domestic business investment.' The authors cited the rightwing Heritage Foundation, which claims that regulation costs US business $2 trillion a year. They urged Trump to decrease the regulatory 'burden' by at least 10 per cent.[2]

But the TTIP drafts were already bad enough. The draft of TTIP's 'Cross-border Trade in Services' chapter is especially far-reaching. One Article states that 'neither Party shall... adopt or maintain... measures that... impose limitations on... the number of service suppliers whether in the form of numerical quotas, monopolies, exclusive service suppliers, or the requirement of an economic needs test'. There is already a decline in European investment banking and a significant increase in US operations. This Chapter of TTIP or a similar one included in any bilateral deal, like the proposed US-UK free trade agreement, could make it easier for US companies to make foreign financial markets more prone to instability and ultimately collapse ('boom-bust').[3]

Since the financial crisis of 2008, the US market share of investment banks in the EU has increased while Europe's has declined. Two experts cite the possibility of Europe's 'complete dependence on US investment banks', especially in the City of London, adding that they are 'on the verge of taking over pole position'. The authors refer to credit-rating agencies and investment banks as 'the gatekeepers of capital markets'. Further withdrawal of EU investment banks from the global market will lead to a monopoly by US firms – Goldman Sachs (which now practically runs the Trump cabinet), Morgan Stanley, JP Morgan, Citigroup and Bank of America Merrill Lynch being the 'bulge bracket'.[4]

This will lead to a 'four-tier investment banking system', the first of which consists of the bulge brackets. The second will comprise 'strong regional players', including Barclays, Deutsche Bank and the Rothschild Group. The investment arms of banks will be the third tier. The fourth will be specialist advisers and wealth managers. 'The US investment banks prefer to deal with one regulator for their European operations.' Discussed below is the fact that many EU banks worry that the US is raising protectionist barriers while insisting that its own institutions receive privileged status.[5]

Let us now turn to the financial crisis in order to explore the importance of regulation in preventing economic shocks.

'Wall Street got drunk'

One of the problems of the US financial sector is its high-risk, high-debt, high-payoff structure buttressed by government insurance policies known as 'too big to fail' – or too big to *jail*, in the words of US Attorney General Loretta Lynch. The high payoffs are for Chief Executive Officers (CEOs), not for the taxpayers who bail them out when their gravy train derails.[6]

From 1978 to 2007, financial-sector debt increased from $3 trillion to $36 trillion. By 1980, financial-sector profits accounted for 15 per cent of all corporate profits. By 2005, they accounted for nearly 30 per cent. In brief, Wall Street was given far too much power. Wall Street companies changed from being private partnerships to publicly traded giants which took increasingly large and diverse risks. In 1990, the 10 largest US financial institutions held about a quarter of the industry's assets. By 2005, that share had reached 55 per cent. With regard to the 2008 financial crisis, 'What else could one expect on a highway where there were neither speed limits nor neatly painted lines?', ask the authors of the US 'Financial Crisis Inquiry Report' (2011). As President George W Bush put it: 'Wall Street got drunk'.[7]

The report notes that '30 years of deregulation and reliance on self-regulation', championed by Federal Reserve Chair Alan Greenspan, successive Congresses and sector lobbyists 'stripped away safeguards'. The industry spent nearly $4 trillion lobbying policymakers and spending on their election campaigns in the decade prior to the collapse. The Securities and Exchange Commission failed to limit derivatives ('financial weapons of mass destruction' as multibillionaire Warren Buffett calls them), the Federal Reserve refused to restrain the actions of liquidity firms and Congress chose not to regulate against what the FBI in 2004 called an 'epidemic in mortgage fraud' largely perpetrated by lenders.[8]

The report concludes that the five biggest investment banks (Bear Stearns, Goldman Sachs, Lehman Brothers, Merrill Lynch and Morgan Stanley) had leverage ratios of 40:1, meaning that for every $40 in assets, they had just $1 in capital to cover their losses. 'Less than a three-per-cent drop in asset values could wipe out a firm.' Indeed, Bear Stearns (later acquired by JPMorgan Chase) and Lehman Brothers (bought by Barclays, Nomura and L3 Communications) sank. Merrill Lynch was saved by an acquisition from Bank of America. The surviving banks were not only saved by government bailouts but their CEOs were rewarded for their catastrophic risks with huge bonuses.[9]

The CEOs learned that crime pays. No major CEOs were prosecuted over the crisis. However, 35 bankers from smaller state banks went to prison over the major fraud (which also included accounting fraud). A report by the London School of Economics five years after the crisis found that, as average wages declined for most working people, the 'top 10 per cent of bankers saw their wages rise by an average 8.6 per cent over the three years, more than the 2.3-per-cent rise for the top decile of all workers'.[9]

In 2016, PricewaterhouseCoopers (PwC) noted a 'seven-year high' in concerns by CEOs about the 'over-regulation' of business and finance by governments. It is understandable that CEOs worry about regulation: their profits and obscene bonuses come from taxpayers. Drawing on data from researchers at the International Monetary Fund (IMF) and Mainz University, the editorial board of *Bloomberg Businessweek* concludes that 'the largest US banks aren't really profitable at all... The billions of dollars they allegedly earn for their shareholders were almost entirely a gift from US taxpayers', who subsidize them to the tune of about $83 billion per annum. 'The top five banks (JPMorgan, Bank of America Corp, Citigroup, Wells Fargo & Co and Goldman Sachs) take most of the profits ($64 billion).' These banks control the bulk of the $9 trillion in assets which make up half the US economy and would collapse 'in the absence of corporate welfare'.[10]

These and other institutions were hoping to use TPP and other multilateral deals to continue the globalization of risky financial markets, which could spell future disaster in emerging economies. Under Trump's bilateral agenda, their dream is still alive.

Europe's collapse

The UK banks Bradford and Bingley and HBOS collapsed in the wake of the 2008 financial crisis. According to a paper by Culpepper and Reinke, Bradford and Bingley's deposits were transferred to another bank by a form of government nationalization. Following a government-granted waiver of competition rules, HBOS merged with Lloyds. The five remaining major banks were Barclays, RBS, HSBC, Standard Chartered and Lloyds. Barclays, HSBC and Standard Chartered remained private, whereas Lloyds and Royal Bank of Scotland (RBS) took Bank of England cash injections. They were 'nationalized in all but name', to quote Mervyn King, at the time Governor of the Bank of England. Under the government's Asset Protection Scheme, the taxpayer lost money in bailing out RBS and Lloyds.[11]

In terms of proportion of GDP, Britain 'spent far more on the bailouts' than France and Germany. The OECD average for bailouts was 9.8 per cent of GDP, including asset relief, credit guarantees and recapitalization. France spent the lowest on bank bailouts at 3.7 per cent; the US, 5.8 per cent; Switzerland, 6.8 per cent; Germany, 8.2 per cent; and the UK, a staggering 21.1 per cent of GDP. According to the National Audit Office, between 2007 and 2010, the British government spent £1.16 trillion ($1.52 trillion) on bailouts, including but not limited to protecting deposits.[12]

In Germany, Deutsche Bank (which makes most of its money outside Germany) opposed nationalization, with the result that Commerzbank, Hypo Real Estate and West LB received bailouts resulting in 'large losses' to the German taxpayer. The six banks operating in France 'enjoy a close relationship with the state'. They were brought into the French government's liquidity fund, with the largest solvent bank, Crédit Mutuel, dependent on domestic revenues, unlike HSBC in the UK and Deutsche Bank in Germany. Dependence on domestic markets forced Crédit Mutuel to accept part-nationalization. 'The United Kingdom and Germany failed to force their preferred terms on the largest banks', say Culpepper and Reinke, 'because HSBC and Deutsche Bank were insufficiently dependent on domestic markets'.[13]

When a financial institution makes most of its money

providing services to domestic markets, including depositors and businesses, it is essentially under government control. When a financial institution is reliant on foreign markets, it can threaten to leave its country of origin, effectively holding the domestic government to ransom. This happened in Germany with Deutsche Bank and in the UK with HSBC. France's Crédit Mutuel, on the other hand, was part-nationalized by the government after the financial crisis because more than 90 per cent of its revenue came from domestic trade. Financial institutions like Crédit Mutuel are a threat to US global designs because governments have a degree of sovereign control over them.[14]

Trump's bilateral FTAs will seek to lower barriers to trade and investment and possibly acquisitions, meaning that if European financial institutions like Crédit Mutuel start trading more with foreign (that is, US) markets, national governments will lose their degree of sovereignty (because the newly internationalized financial institution can threaten to relocate), becoming less sustainable for national governments and more profitable for US institutions.

The financial crisis affected poorly regulated markets, mainly the US and Britain, but also better regulated markets, such as those of France and Germany. Part of the dangers of interdependence are the gilt and bond markets, which financial institutions and governments needlessly move into. The government issues gilts to fund its activities and the private sector buys them.[15] Gilts are a safe investment because cost is deferred to the taxpayer.*

Susan George points out that, where the poorest Eurozone economies (Greece, Ireland, Portugal, Spain) were concerned, Troika loans (from the European Commission, European

---

* By 2011, the UK was €7.3 trillion ($8.5tn) in debt to other countries' banks (or 436 per cent of foreign debt to GDP): €578.6 billion ($676bn) was owed to the US; €379.3bn ($443bn) to Germany; €316.6bn ($370bn) to Spain; €209.9bn ($245bn) to France; €122.7bn ($143.3bn) to Japan; and €113.5bn ($132.5bn) to Ireland. France's foreign debt was less than the UK's at €4.2 trillion ($4.9tn) or 235 per cent of GDP of which: €227 billion ($265bn) was owed to the UK; €202.1bn ($236.1bn) to the US; and €123.5bn ($144.3bn) to Germany. Germany's foreign debt was €4.2 trillion ($4.9tn, or 176 per cent of GDP), of which: €205.8 billion ($240.5bn) was owed to France; €202.7bn ($236.9bn) to Italy; €174.4bn ($203.8bn) to the US; and €141.1bn ($164.9bn) to the UK.[16]

Central Bank and International Monetary Fund) were packaged as profitable euro bonds, as opposed to lower-interest German or French bonds, hence more profitable to lenders. The money for servicing the debts had to come from somewhere. The easiest targets were the poor – the least educated, the least politically influential and the easiest to attack with teargas, rubber bullets and media propaganda. Technocrats/caretaker governments soon came to power in Europe, including Bulgaria's Plamen Oresharski, the Czech Republic's Jan Fischer, Greece's Lucas Papademos, Italy's Mario Monti and Hungary's Gordon Bajnai.[17]

Many fail, but European states are committed to maintaining national deficits under 3 per cent of GDP (or maintaining a 60-per-cent national debt to GDP ratio). This has given governments an excuse to impose austerity. Austria cut €1.6 billion ($1.8bn) in public services. The Czech Republic cut 10 per cent of its budget. France cut €45 billion ($52.5bn) over three years. Germany cut €30 billion ($35bn) over four years from social spending. Greece cut 25 per cent from public-sector wages. Ireland cut social welfare by €760 million ($888m) in addition to a €16 ($19) per child monthly benefit reduction. Portugal privatized 17 public enterprises. In the UK, €83 billion ($97bn) was cut from public spending over four years, nearly half a million public-sector workers were made redundant and long-term unemployment benefit was reduced by 15 per cent.[18]

'Capitalizing on crisis'

The financial crisis of 2008 and Troika-arranged austerity plunged an extra 7.5 million Europeans into poverty, where they joined 120 million others who were already in poverty. (These figures exclude the UK because British monetary policy is set by the Bank of England, not EU institutions.) Per-capita income in the European Union could, assuming equal wealth distribution, equate to €26,600 ($31,000) per annum. As it stands, wealth is unequally distributed. The European Union's GDP is €4.5 trillion ($52.6tn). The EU is home to (depending on the year) 340 billionaires, who own €1.3 trillion ($1.5tn) – over a quarter of the EU's wealth. Governments 'dismantled the mechanisms that reduce inequality and enable equitable growth', wrote Oxfam in a 2013 report. Notice that policymakers are committed to growth, but not to equitable growth; as three Citigroup analysts put it, 'the few [must] retain that fatter profit share', or as two Royal Institute for International Affairs authors suggest, the 'international system' is 'structured in ways which perpetuate those privileges'. Oxfam concludes that 'the poorest have been hit hardest, as the burden of responsibility for the excesses of past decades is passed to those most vulnerable and least to blame'.[19]

It is also worth noting that, at the international level, there is no law stating that workers' hard-earned money has to be handed over to bailing out financial institutions at the expense of social policies which, the UN reminds governments, they are committed to upholding.[20]

Having targeted the poor, Brussels received enormous applause from major institutions like the World Economic Forum (Davos). Kalin Anev Janse, Secretary General of the European Stability Mechanism (ESM), wrote an article for Davos. (The ESM receives policy advice from private consultancy firms, which often own shares in it.) Janse's article is titled, 'How the financial crisis made Europe stronger'. The title might seem a little odd, even absurd, to casual readers. But when read through, the elite thinking makes perfect sense. Europe is 'strong' in that economic 'growth' is picking up again: never mind that 'growth' is mainly in the financial sector, of which 80 per cent does not contribute to the real economy (labour, production, consumption, etc). The fanatical devotion to 'growth' and its relation to deficit reduction is very unequally distributed, as noted above. Ergo, it is 'growth' for a very narrow sector of the population: the 'plutocracy', as Citigroup describes them.[21]

Janse writes that 'Europe not only endured the last crisis, it capitalized upon it'. Under some new initiatives, taxpayer money will supposedly not be needed (though no evidence is provided), unlike the current 'need for the public sector to use taxpayers' money for economic and financial shock absorption'. In Davos language, 'unsustainable government policies' means socialist(ic) programmes of spending on state pensions, social security, education and so forth. Janse denounces socialist policies for producing 'bloated pre-crisis wages'. But 'bloated wages' refers only to labourers, state-sector workers, and so on, not the 'bloated wages' of Europe's CEOs and billionaires. Janse describes the callous attack on the poor as 'courageous decisions' made by brave governments. Janse also notes that, although banks kept interest rates low to stimulate lending, they did so in the most roundabout way: where central banks bought private bonds with 'unlimited liquidity'. The poorest countries, Greece, Ireland, Portugal and Spain, earned the title 'reform champions', says Janse, by 'improving their public finances, reducing deficits, and cutting labour costs to make themselves more competitive'. Meanwhile, about 40 per cent of Greeks lived in poverty, with a quarter of Greek children attending school without breakfast or lunch.[22]

The 2008 financial crisis compelled European states to regulate their markets more efficiently. Banks are 'preoccupied with divergence in financial market regulation and the costs that regulatory fragmentation can bring'. According to the European Parliamentary Research Services (EPRS), financial services constitute about 48 per cent of all EU exports to the US (excluding insurance). One of the obstacles to liberalization and harmonization is the familiar one of 'Strong regulatory autonomy' – in other words, national independence. The US wants to deregulate EU protection. As the EPRS report says: 'the US will want a strong commitment to financial market liberalization within TTIP', as well as within bilateral deals, but 'will oppose anything that might impose a limitation on their regulatory autonomy in the field'. In the US, the Volcker Rule protects banks and other financial institutions from self-harm by preventing traders from using their firm's money to trade bonds, commodities, currencies, derivatives and stocks, but allows them to use depositors' money. It is a barrier against penetration by foreign firms.[23]

'Corporate capture'

In 2011, Euro-American chambers of commerce wrote to the White House and to the EU's trade commissioner, advising the abandonment of sovereignty and a 'general approach' to guaranteeing US investor rights in host nations, 'apply[ing] the widest possible definition of investments, including all forms of assets and tangible and intangible property; property rights such as leases, mortgages, liens and pledges... business enterprises and equity and other forms of participation in them'.[24]

When TTIP (though not its details) was made public, the European Commission orchestrated a careful propaganda campaign, publishing vague statements on what the current rounds of negotiations involved. One paper talks about state-owned enterprises (SOEs), which are a threat to private corporations. The paper in question states: 'SOEs (and sometimes even private companies) may enjoy privileges and immunities that are not available to competitors, thereby giving them undue competitive advantage over their rivals.' As a result, the state must be divorced from owning its resources. Another paper states: 'The parties [to TTIP] could reflect on the feasibility to prohibit certain types of subsidies', such as subsidies for health, housing, education and so on, lest these constitute market interference.[25]

The secrecy surrounding TTIP made it hard to find direct evidence about motives and tactics from financial institutions and their representatives. Some direct evidence does exist. One striking piece is from JPMorgan Chase. 'The TPP and TTIP seem to be about corporate capture', says the report, which is worth quoting at length. 'With global trade negotiations deadlocked for years, regional agreements – long a dormant route to trade liberalization – are back with a vengeance.' The TPP and TTIP put the US 'at the center of two megadeals that could shape the future path of world trade'. The author of the report generally agrees with the NAFTA model examined in the appendix, and concludes that 'trade agreements do not create jobs; they simply reallocate them across industries'.[26]

Lowering barriers is said by TTIP advocates to increase exports, but also to promote specialization. These are 'mutually contradictory' objectives, the report continues, but a contradiction arises only if one believes the 'free market' propaganda. In the real world, if the US is essentially exporting to its own captive markets, raising barriers to prevent others from doing the same, it is not impeding its own growth. As the author puts it: 'Trade agreements can create jobs, but only to the extent that they destroy jobs in other countries.' As two Royal Institute for International Affairs authors point out, it is 'politically much easier' to blame the abstractions of the market than to be honest about political choices. The JPMorgan Chase author concludes that 'either argument' for lowering trade barriers (ie importing) or mercantilism (ie protecting against imports) is 'inconsistent with their advocates' key claim that such deals will simultaneously create jobs and be mutually beneficial'. The author regards it as 'strange...' that advocates of TTIP 'simultaneously rely on both arguments'.[27]

In 2015, a chapter of TTIP was leaked to the media. Over a hundred pages in length, it is titled, 'Trade in Services and Investment Schedule of Specific Commitments and Reservations'. Governments had different concerns, depending on their unique positions, and so they added clauses specific to their countries. Part I, 'Horizontal Commitments', Section A, discusses 'commercial presences' (such as US banks) and 'limitations on national treatment' (such as deregulation) as a boon to US outsourcing. It states that 'foreign investments in France in sectors listed in article R153-2 of the financial and monetary code' – relating to the privatization of public health and other financial institutions – 'are subject to prior approval from the Minister for the Economy'. This means that if the US puts pressure on the French ministry or threatens an ISDS case, sovereign measures could erode. In an apparent effort to pre-empt this, France expanded its domestic powers in the financial and monetary code amendments in 2014.[28]

Financial markets and the dangers of 'free trade'

The US Census Bureau points out that, following the financial crisis, the country's poverty rate 'has actually increased in 12 states. The nation's overall poverty rate was 14.8 per cent, which means 46.7 million people were living in poverty in 2014.' One European Commission paper on TTIP explains that public procurement in TTIP will enable 'EU firms to bid for more public contracts in the US... For public authorities with tight budgets, it can bring: better value for money; more choice; greater economic efficiency.'[29]

Certain provisions in the financial regulations at the World Trade Organization allow governments to retain some controls over the movement of capital. But TTIP or legislation in similar 'free trade' agreements could undermine this. By giving discretionary powers to states, the General Agreement on Trade in Services (GATS) clause restricts capital movement, with the exception of temporary measures concerning balance-of-payment problems. Under ISDSs, which are likely to be incorporated into TTIP, governments that exercise regulatory prudence (thereby interfering with US operational freedoms) may find themselves sued.[30]

The financial aspects of TTIP date back to the Financial Market Regulatory Dialogue 2002, which included the US Treasury, Federal Reserve, Securities and Exchange Commission and Commodity Futures Trading Commission, the same bodies that were largely responsible for the crisis in 2008. On the European side, it included the European Commission and European Supervisory Authorities (the Banking Authority, Insurance and Occupational Pensions Authority and Securities and Markets Authority). The European Banking Federation represents corporations that account for 80 per cent of assets, deposits and loans in the EU; it 'strongly supports' arrangements being negotiated for TTIP and recommends that the Financial Market Regulatory Dialogue 'be improved and incorporated into the framework of the TTIP regulatory chapter'.[31]

Together, US and EU banks constitute 55 per cent of world banking assets and 80 per cent of the derivatives business. The US has $430 billion 'directly' invested in EU financial markets and the EU $330 billion in the US. Financial services account for 4.8 per cent of US GDP ($720 billion) and include commercial banks, non-depository intermediators, financial advisory services (such as portfolio management and investment advice), security brokers and savings banks. Current US financial exports to the EU are 36 per cent. They grew by just over two per cent following the financial crisis.[32]

Like insurance, 'US financial services exports face a variety of non-tariff measures that restrict access to the EU market', says the British government. Non-tariff measures constitute just over 11 per cent of hidden or *de facto* tariffs on US exports. By 2025, 'US financial services exports to the EU will grow by almost six per cent from 2011 levels'. Where will the six per cent go? It is likely that healthcare and social security will be financialized, as will private and state pensions, especially with an ex-Rothschild banker in power in France and a neoliberal Brexit under way in the UK.[33]

Insurance: 'spreading risk globally'

The European Commission was adamant that 'international standards' in relation to regulation of financial markets occur 'outside' TTIP, meaning that, even though the deal is essentially dead, the core structures are already in place.[34]

Shortly after the election of the Conservatives in the UK in 2015, the Confederation of British Industry (CBI) met to hear a speech by its then President, Sir Mike Rake, who said that the European Commission's body for financing start-ups and non-listed entities, the Capital Markets Union, 'shows signs... of unlocking the potential of financial services right across the EU', including insurance and reinsurance. The City of London Corporation is 'Europe's financial capital', says Rake, who noted that 'the City needs Europe as a gateway to clients, business and investment' – hence the need for a post-Brexit open market.[35]

Lloyds brags that it 'is active in promoting the benefits of free trade and removal of regulatory and market barriers to (re)insurance'. It goes on to explain: 'Submissions to national and international policymakers and meetings with key government representatives are some of the tools we use to draw policymakers' attention on trade barriers in insurance and reinsurance'. Lloyds laments the 'increasing worldwide trend for reinsurance protectionism' and the 'barriers to the transfer of risks through global reinsurance markets'. 'Transfer of risk' is an interesting turn of phrase: risk is transferred to the public, benefit is transferred to the rich. Protectionism limits the reinsurer's ability 'to spread risk globally'. Sovereignty also means exclusion by privileging domestic insurers.[36]

There are very few barriers to financial trade between the US and EU. The main obstacles are informal barriers, known as non-tariff barriers. Tom Stephenson of the financial advisory group Robus described non-tariff barriers as 'differences in regulatory standards'.[37]

US and EU companies represent 61 per cent of worldwide premiums. Under an FTA, US insurance service exports will grow by 10 per cent. The US insurance sector is worth $440 billion or 2.9 per cent of US GDP. It includes pensions, life, health, property, property insurance carriers and reinsurance agencies, brokerages and carriers. Only $3.5 billion are currently exports, of which the European Union is a relatively small market (23 per cent). The government reckons that non-tariff measures amount to a 10.8 per cent equivalent tariff on US insurance exports. By 2027, removal of these barriers will increase, amounting to zero or near-zero tariffs for the US.[38]

The Insurance Europe federation 'welcomes' the idea of an FTA with the US, citing economic integration and regulatory co-operation as a measure of potential growth. '(Re)insurance is a fundamental ingredient for creating a robust economy', they say, complaining: 'Insurance is a highly regulated sector and insurers frequently find themselves subject to costly duplicative regulatory requirements'. One of the purposes of the World Trade Organization is to set rules that non-members are forced to follow. Insurance Europe writes that insurance-related policies will 'influence the shape of global (re)insurance supervision and regulation'. WTO's GATS framework establishes financial services policy. Insurance Europe wants to 'go... beyond the commitments' of GATS.[39]

According to the US federal government's investigation into the financial crisis, high leverage ratios were a major cause of the crisis. Banking, insurance and financial institutions had no collateral except taxpayer bailouts to guard against downturn. In spite of this, Insurance Europe says it 'has long opposed collateral requirements in the US', describing them as 'a discriminatory market access barrier'. Protection against disaster is, according to this view, a market barrier, much in the way that producing food domestically to guard against hunger or, for tobacco companies, telling people that smoking is bad for them, is tantamount to market interference. Insurance Europe calls for the 'total elimination' of collateral requirements in US markets.[40]

Insurance Europe notes a number of US tax reliefs for foreign (re)insurance companies, including the Neil Bill of 2010 and the Senate Finance Committees' tax reform proposals, and laments the risk of 'double taxation' in these reforms, which gives some idea about what an FTA or a series of bilateral FTAs with the US will really mean for European insurance companies.[41]

US-EU tensions: 'beggar thy neighbour'

Businesses on both sides of the Atlantic were unhappy about compromises in TTIP, especially in the financial regulations sector. This is because European banks and other financial institutions worry that TTIP would liberalize European markets, allowing US firms to act as they wish, all the while maintaining protectionist clauses in the US, constraining the decisions of European financial institutions abroad. European policymakers are ambivalent about the financial (de)regulation clauses in TTIP. On the one hand, European financial institutions (including banks and insurers) want a market liberal enough to profit from exotic products, such as derivatives, but on the other they want protection from rival US companies and the ability to operate with a degree of freedom in the US.

In a letter to the American Federal Reserve, the Association of German Banks (AGB, an organization which represents over 200 private banks) complains about Sections 165 and 166 of the US Dodd-Frank Act because it 'would unduly constrain US activities for German and other non-US banks'. After the 'single market' of the EU, most German investment is with the US. AGB is worried that Dodd-Frank's 'nationalistic approach would lead to... an excessive operational burden... produc[ing] significant broader costs for the financial sectors and economies affected'. In other words, the US is raising barriers against too much penetration and control by foreign banks while pushing for liberalization in Europe. The letter refers to this as a 'beggar-thy-neighbour' policy.[42]

Dodd-Frank requires the US Federal Reserve to interrogate banks with over $50 billion in assets. At the time of writing, under one per cent of US banks have global assets of that amount. The AGB describes this clause as 'unduly extraterritorial'. So, when the AGB expresses concern for its constituents, it is primarily referring to the largest German banks, which hold more than $50 billion in *global* assets. 'While we have not actively pleaded for reciprocal action with our regulators,' the AGB continues, referring to German and Brussels-level policymakers, 'such reactions may well be caused if the proposed rule were to become final rulemaking.' The AGB writes that 'any bilateral negotiations... [should encourage] mutual recognition of comparable standards'.[43]

The European Banking Federation, which represents over 4,500 banks, also wrote to the Federal Reserve, complaining that the US's Intermediate Holding Company structure will subject foreign banks and their subsidiaries operating in the US to restrictive liquidity requirements. The EBF argues that this runs counter to Section 165 of Dodd-Frank. Such 'discriminat[ion]' will harm 'efficient global financial markets', meaning the operational freedoms of European banks in the US. Like the AGB, the EBF is concerned that 'liquidity will be effectively trapped in the US'. Just as the AGB fears 'beggar-thy-neighbour', the EBF raises concerns about a non-level playing field. The EBF also cautions that non-US banks might retaliate by raising protectionist barriers against US companies operating in Europe. To avoid such a standoff, the EBF and the AGB advocate co-operation through FTAs.[44]

The US responded to these threats by announcing that it would exclude financial (de)regulation from 'free trade' negotiations. This put the financial rounds into stalemate, as regulatory harmonization could not be reached.[45]

In draft texts, the European framers attempted to include provisions to safeguard domestic control over regulation, which seemed to go against their call for equality. Article 3(1) of the draft chapter on 'Trade in Services, Investment and E-Commerce', for instance, reads: 'Each Party shall accord in its territory to covered investments of the other Party and investors with respect to their covered investments fair and equitable treatment and full protection and security'. Article 5(1) even retains the possibility of nationalizing securities '(a) for a public purpose' (which is undefined), meaning that the threat of nationalization has been included in the draft as a shield against broad US demands. The shield is rather weak, however, as Article 3 makes provisions for 'compensation... amount[ing] to the fair market value of the investment at the [given] time'. Another provision discusses 'public debt', suggesting ways of transferring risk and cost to the public sector.[46]

10 Healthcare: 'Selling splints to Europe'

How US 'free trade' deals will hurt Europe's healthcare systems and help to complete the decades-long process of privatizing Britain's renowned National Health Service.

Europeans enjoy free healthcare. Each system is different. Britain's National Health Service (NHS) is funded by National Insurance. The French pay for about a third of their healthcare, and, except in specific circumstances (such as cases of patients with long-term disabilities), the government subsidizes the rest. Germany has a mandatory health insurance fund, as well as a private one. Polls suggest that Europeans are determined to continue with free healthcare. It is not clear which country has the best system. That depends on what comparative measures are used. The Commonwealth Fund uses as its measures process, access, administrative efficiency, equity and outcomes. The admittedly 'free market' Legatum Institute uses overall physical and mental health, the ability to prevent illness and hospital infrastructure. In 2017, the Commonwealth Fund found that Britain has the best overall healthcare system, while the Legatum Institute put Britain in 20th place.[1]

One thing that almost everyone agrees on, however, is that the US model is the worst; it is regularly rated at or near the bottom of all the so-called developed nations. Healthcare in the US is almost entirely privatized, minus state subsidies for giant corporations, like drug companies. One of the few good policies implemented under Obama was the Affordable Care Act of 2010 (ACA). The ACA did not go far enough, but it did provide some insurance coverage for the very poorest Americans. Nobody in Europe wants the US model, except the very few who have enough money to pay for all their health needs. The US remains the world's superpower, both economically (in terms of GDP) and militarily. It sets – or at least tries to set – economic policy and norms for the rest of the world to follow. It is, therefore, important to understand the US healthcare model if we are to safeguard against its possible exportation to Europe, including to the United Kingdom.

The way in which the US model could be exported to Europe is through bilateral or multilateral 'free trade' agreements. As members of the European Union, individual EU states are safe from US-led bilateral agreements because *individual* states are not permitted to sign 'free trade' deals. However, it is possible that the EU *as a whole* could sign a deal (such as TTIP) with the US. It is likely that, if the UK leaves the EU, it will sign 'free trade' deals with the US, some of which could involve further erosion of the NHS. Legislation to privatize or open up to insurance providers could be introduced, for example.

The US healthcare model

US health insurers frequently find excuses and loopholes to deny coverage and revoke existing coverage in order to retain their capital and maximize profits. A survey carried out by the New York State Medical Society in 2008 found that 90 per cent of New York physicians felt pressured by insurance companies to change the ways in which they diagnose and treat patients. In cases involving potential high insurance payouts by companies to cover medical costs, such as cancer diagnoses, insurers write to doctors demanding that the given ailment be re-diagnosed as something less serious – and thus less expensive. Ninety-two per cent of physicians agreed that incentives and disincentives suggested by insurance companies (depending on the given case) were in the worst interests of patients. Eighty-seven per cent of respondents said they felt pressured to prescribe treatments based on costs, not care. The survey concluded that 93 per cent of respondents confirmed insurers had even 'required' them to change prescriptions.[2]

US health insurance companies employ teams of investigators who have or gain access to claimants' private medical records and scrutinize every page for alleged false statements. The US House Subcommittee on Oversight and

Investigations revealed that the insurance companies Assurant, UnitedHealth Group and WellPoint Inc saved $300 million by cancelling 20,000 Americans' health-insurance policies. The Committee found that policyholders, representing a total of over 1,000 illnesses (including cancer), were targeted for the retroactive cancellation of policies known as rescission. In one case, a woman's coverage for breast cancer was revoked because she failed to disclose to the insurer that she had once been treated for acne. Over a six-year period, Health Net saved $35 million through rescissions and, like other companies, actually incentivized them by offering employees bonuses for reaching rescission targets.[3]

Between 2007 and 2010, 12 million Americans were either denied overall health coverage by insurance companies, refused care for specific conditions, or priced out by high premium costs. According to a US Congressional investigation, between the years 2007 and 2009 alone America's four largest health insurance companies (Aetna, Humana, UnitedHealth Group and WellPoint) denied cover to at least 651,000 individuals because of their previous medical conditions. This amounts to one in seven applications being denied. Previous health 'conditions' used by insurance companies to justify rescissions included pregnancy. It would seem that the industry knew of the Democratic-controlled Congress's decision to attempt to pass laws prohibiting denial of coverage based on previous conditions because denials and rescissions in that two-year period rose by 49 per cent.[4]

Threats to European healthcare

There are already high-level EU plans to push through privatization. In a letter to Lord Livingston, Conservative Minister for Trade and Investment in 2015, EU Trade Commissioner Cecilia Malmström wrote that, despite empty assurances to the public that 'trade' agreement clauses will enable governments to retain control over healthcare, there is a 'thriving private market for health services in the EU. This sector is a key European strength', partly because of state subsidies to private firms, like the UK's appalling private finance initiatives (PFI) schemes (see note 5) and partly because Europe has an excellent health record compared with the US. Malmström stated that 'it is important that EU trade policy helps to enable our health services companies to access international markets such as the US, as well as to encourage competition on the EU side.' Malmström went on to note how the European Commission's Director General for Trade, Ignacio Garcia Bercero, 'explained ... that health services are within the scope of EU trade policy [and] to ensure that sectors are not ruled out unnecessarily'.[5]

The real and evident advantages that European healthcare systems have over the US need to be defended against attempts by EU bureaucrats and their post-Brexit counterparts in the UK to lay the groundwork for further privatization. EU documents emphasize, for example, the importance of government 'predictability' – by which is meant their consistency in being open to privatization.

So what are the existing European systems that are under threat? Under German law, citizens are required to have medical insurance. Germany's 'sickness funds' are private, not-for-profit insurance companies, which collect premiums from employers and their employees. Germany has public health insurance for workers who experience work-related illness and injury. Organized by German Social Accident Insurance, it provides cover to 3.8 million companies and institutions and 76 million individuals. In addition, the Social Insurance for Agriculture, Forestry and Landscaping provides accident cover to sector workers. Compared with the US, Germany spends less on hi-tech medical equipment, such as MRIs, and more on accessibility. In the US, there are thousands of MRI machines, but millions of patients who cannot afford to use them. The US system epitomizes high-expense, low-outcome spending.[6]

As in France, German physicians are paid less than their US counterparts. However, of all OECD countries, Germans visit GPs more, are prescribed more drugs (as opposed to buying them based on marketing pressures), stay longer in hospital and have higher admissions. In 1990, 100,000 German students were attending state-run medical schools. Following six years of education, students spent five more years in training.

A poll in 1990 found that 60 per cent of Americans were dissatisfied with the state of healthcare, believing that it required major structural changes. Polling analysts conclude that the unaffordability and low quality of insurance coverage (where it is available) is a major reason for widespread despair over the US system. By comparison only 5 per cent of Canadians said that their national system required major changes, and just 13 per cent of Germans thought their system needed complete rebuilding.[7]

As of 2002, France was spending under 10 per cent of its GDP on health, yet had one of the best systems in the world. The US was then spending over 13 per cent of GDP on health and had (and still has) one of the worst systems in the 'developed' world. The US spends more on health per capita than France. A review by the Brookings Institution maintains that access to health insurance is a reason for the disparity. In the US and France, medical care is funded by workers through gross wage premiums. In the US, health insurance is a flat rate, whereas in France it is adjusted for income. The French pay for about 13 per cent of their personal healthcare out of their own pockets while private insurers account for 12 per cent. However, 74 per cent is covered by public-private funds (the rest is covered by national and local government contributions). Doctors' fees in France are effectively limited by insurers who resist paying out high rates.[8]

in the US, until the Affordable Care Act came along, the private-insurance industry dominated and continues to have a massive influence over US healthcare, with 35 per cent of coverage from private funds, 17 per cent from clients and 43 per cent from government sources. France uses public hospitals and salaried staff, whereas the US frequently uses local medical centres that are linked to education and research and rely on interns. In the US, much of the exorbitant waste goes on the salaries of doctors, who earn five times more than the average worker; in France, physicians earn twice the amount of the average worker. French doctors generally enter their profession with little debt, paying less liability insurance.[9]

As in the European cases cited above, Canadians have universal healthcare and spend less on hi-tech machines and physicians' salaries. The US Bureau of Economic Research concludes that the Canadian system 'seems to do more for less', while one in five of those aged under 60 in the US remain uninsured. By 2016, Canada was spending 10.4 per cent of GDP on healthcare, compared with 16 per cent expenditure in the US (up from 13 per cent in 2002). A Gallup poll from 2003 compared the attitudes of Canadians with those of Britons and Americans: 57 per cent of Canadians and 43 per cent of Britons expressed satisfaction 'with the availability of affordable healthcare'. By comparison, '44 per cent of Americans are very dissatisfied with the availability of affordable healthcare, and nearly three-fourths (72 per cent) are either somewhat or very dissatisfied'. In the United States, '25 per cent are satisfied with the availability of affordable healthcare, but 48 per cent are satisfied with quality'.[10]

Researchers Eger and Mahlich write that in Europe, government control over healthcare 'is indeed associated with lower drug prices and consecutively with lower health expenditures' compared with the US. A 2014 report by the OECD ranked the quality of US private healthcare lowest of all industrialized Western nations, with European countries – which have universal healthcare – dominating the top 10. In the US, Medicare is a programme initiated in the 1960s for the retired and younger disabled. It uses approximately 30 private insurance companies and covers 48 per cent of patients' costs. The Medicare bureaucracy is legally prevented from seeking lower drug costs despite being the biggest buyer of drugs. This amounts to a form of government protection for Big Pharma. Per-capita drug spending in the US is 40 per cent higher than in Canada, 75 per cent higher than in Japan and 300 per cent higher than in Denmark.[11]

Americans not only fail to benefit from these high prices, but their taxes also subsidize cheaper European drug purchases. The US subsidizes 46 per cent of research and development in the life sciences globally, according to R&D magazine.[12] Mick Kolassa of Medical Marketing Economics says that European governments threaten to close the market to US pharmaceutical firms if prices go too high. On the whole, governments in Europe tend to set drug prices whereas, in the US, this is effectively done by the pharmaceutical industry. Professor Jacob Sherkow of the New York Law School concludes that when it comes to drug prices, 'US consumers are in fact subsidizing other countries' public health systems'. He might have added that they are also subsidizing their own, twice: once through research programmes and again by purchasing private healthcare. Kolassa said that it is 'not fair' that French patients, for example, pay less for US-developed drugs than US patients. 'But there's not much we can do about it.'[13]

One thing that can be done, and perhaps will start to happen under a US-led FTA or BIT, is to buy up enough of France's (or any country's) public-health assets and force the price of drugs up to domestic US levels. This book has already discussed the protection of intellectual property, including drugs, for big corporations (the TRIPS agreement). Many activist-researchers fear that TTIP – or some TTIP-esque 'free trade' agreement – could include a kind of TRIPS-plus provision, which could push drug prices even higher than the buy-out of state-owned health assets.

Part of the high price of drugs can be attributed to this technique of making patients pay for pharmaceutical research, convincing them through advertising to buy the given products and then making them pay again out of their own pockets. In fact, research spending is so low within the big pharma companies that between 1998 and 2007 more than 50 per cent of approved US drugs emerged from universities and biotech firms instead. The Congressional Budget Office concludes that government controls on pricing would save the US federal government $137 billion over the next decade.[14]

A brief history of the UK National Health Service

Poll after poll shows overwhelming public support in the UK not only for keeping the NHS in public hands, but for getting it back into public hands. But privateers openly discuss how the NHS will be turned into a publicly funded provider to private insurance companies. In order to make this happen, the system must first become highly inefficient and costly.

The National Health Service has a long history. The Workmen's Compensation Act of 1897 was expanded to universal compensation in 1906. This was followed by compulsory health insurance in 1912 and general unemployment insurance in 1920. The Unemployment Act was passed in 1934, giving some security to the jobless. In 1941, Churchill's government established a Committee on Reconstruction Problems, of which Sir William Beveridge was Chair. The aim was to study social insurance and allied services. The report referred to the War as a 'revolutionary' time, concluding that a 'revolutionary moment in the world's history is a time for revolutions, not for patching'. Instead of 'patching' up the old 19th-century model of 'friendly societies' – decentralized, localized healthcare administered by Boards of Guardians within Local Authorities – the report argued that national social security and healthcare should be established.[15]

This, wrote Beveridge, would form part of the 'social progress', culminating in 'Medical treatment covering all requirements... provided for all citizens by a national health service organized under the health departments and post-medical rehabilitation treatment will be provided for all persons capable of profiting by it'. The NHS was formally created through a series of legislations adopted under Attlee's Labour government, which came to power in 1945. From the outset, certain elements of the NHS were private. GPs are private contractors, not direct civil servants. Prescriptions are charged to those with means. Ophthalmological and dentistry services are, with few exceptions, paid for out-of-pocket.[16]

The Conservatives' 1945 manifesto had envisaged maintaining 'voluntary hospitals' under the control of local authorities, as well as close collaboration with universities, much like the US system is run today. By the third reading of the bill that established the NHS in 1948, the Conservatives were complaining that the Labour version 'discourage[s] voluntary effort and association', writes John Lister. The NHS that came into being under Aneurin Bevan (Labour Minister of Health from 1945 to 1951) permitted the use of state-funded hospitals for private insurance patients, amounting to a subsidy for private health providers. One of the major problems of the NHS from the perspective of the rich was its effect on the private health insurance industry. Prior to World War Two, 10 million Britons (about a third of the population) had private health insurance. By 1950, with the NHS established, 120,000 held private insurance. The Conservatives regularly dreamed up ideas to privatize the NHS. Writing in the *International Medical Tribune* in 1967, for example, Shadow Health Minister Bernard Braine wrote that 'hotel charge[s] for a hospital stay' could be levied against patients,as could 'medical care... charges'.[17]

During the 1980s, the Conservatives forced hundreds of hospitals and clinics to close, introduced targets for bed provisions, increased prescription prices 13-fold in just under a decade and closed mental-health services ('care in the community'). They also dissociated nurses' pay from ancillary work, such as sanitation, laundry and catering, which had the effect of breaking solidarity between nurses and contract staff. In 1992, they established private finance initiatives (PFIs) to lend public money for private hospital construction and management. Under Tony Blair's New Labour, PFIs became even more developed and ran up a debt of over £260 billion ($351 billion).[18]

One of the final nails in the NHS's coffin came in 2012 under the Conservative-Liberal coalition government (which was approximately 80 per cent Conservative). Its White Paper, subtitled 'Liberating the NHS', proudly pledged to cut managerial spending by 45 per cent and overall spending by £20 billion ($26 billion) over four years. The paper framed the NHS as part of the 'Big Society', a scheme to defund charities and social services, turn charities into corporations and rely on volunteerism to provide public services. The paper also discussed devolving power to defunded local authorities, which amounts to privatization. The paper claimed to 'recognize' the 'interdependence' of adult social care services (which are increasingly contracted to private providers) and the NHS. The report also stated that the government 'will seek to break down barriers between health and social care funding', meaning that care costs will be mixed between private providers and subsidizers.[19]

One objective is to impose 'large cuts in administrative costs', meaning that doctors and nurses – as if they don't already have enough to do – will increasingly take on managerial responsibilities. The paper made clear that 'the NHS will employ fewer staff at the end of this Parliament'. It went on: 'Our strategy is about making changes for the long term; not just for this Parliament, but beyond.' Earlier in the chapter it was established that the US overspends on hi-technology and underspends on services and efficiency. The White Paper proposed the government should spend more money on hi-technology to provide real-time patient/doctor feedback. The original Conservative NHS manifesto from 1945 called for reliance on medical training and university-level providers. In 2010 the White Paper reiterated this aim: 'The Department [of Health] will continue to promote the role of Biomedical Research Centres and Units, Academic Health Science Centres and Collaborations for Leadership in Applied Health Research and Care, to develop research and to unlock synergies between research, education and patient care.' The Paper went on to pledge the introduction of performance-based pay, pitting staff in competition with each another.[20]

In October 2010, Mark Britnell, an adviser to Prime Minister David Cameron, attended a conference on the privatization of healthcare. Britnell is Chair of and Senior Partner to the Global Health Practice at KPMG, a tax advisory and auditing firm. Prior to this appointment, Britnell was Director-General for Commissioning and Systems Management at the NHS and Chief Executive of University Hospitals Birmingham, the NHS Foundation and the South Central Strategic Health Authority. The conference was organized by Apax, whose website explains what the organization does: 'Investment executives in each of our four global sector teams – Tech & Telco, Services, Healthcare, and Consumer – are responsible for sourcing and reviewing potential investment opportunities for our funds.' At the conference, referring to burdening GPs with managerial responsibilities, Britnell said: 'Because it is their business, GPs are likely to be far more hard-nosed than the state was in negotiating prices... GPs will have to aggregate purchasing power... and there will be a big opportunity for those companies that can facilitate this process.'[21]

Britnell continued: 'In future, the NHS will be a state insurance provider not a state deliverer... The NHS will be shown no mercy and the best time to take advantage of this will be in the next couple of years' – in other words, during the all-out Conservative assault.[22]

The Health and Social Care Act 2012 was drafted with advice from the private consultancy firm McKinsey and Co. It removed responsibility from the Secretary of State for Health for the first time since the creation of the NHS. The Act abolished Primary Care Trusts and Strategic Health Authorities, replacing them with hundreds of clinical commissioning groups, the managerial responsibility for which is left with GPs. The bill removes caps on the private income sources of NHS Trusts, which it also abolishes and replaces with Foundation Trusts.[23]

Americanizing the NHS: 'The less care they give, the more money they make'

US corporations have sought to infiltrate and acquire the NHS for years. One paper by the US Chamber of Commerce specifically about healthcare is subtitled 'Selling Splints to Europe'. It concerns the regulatory inconveniences posed to small-to-medium-sized US businesses by current standards.[24]

The Tennessee-based Hospital Corporation of America (HCA) already facilitates the use of NHS hospitals for private clients, particularly in specialist areas such as cancer treatment and children's services. In 2015, Britain's private Aspen Healthcare was acquired by the Texas-based Tenet Healthcare. Tenet said that the 'privatization of the UK marketplace, given market inefficiencies and pressures on the National Health Service, should create organic and *de novo* opportunities'. In 2014, Pennsylvania's Universal Health Services acquired the addictions specialist, Cygnet Health. In 2015, the Canada-based Acadia corporation bought the Priory Group. Cygnet/UHS then bought Alpha Hospitals and Acadia/PIC acquired Care UK's mental-health division. Consultancy firm CarterSchwartz notes that takeovers of mental-healthcare providers leapt from 16 in 2014 to 22 in 2015, 'which has left the UK's £16-billion [$21 billion] mental healthcare market bracing itself for a wave of consolidation'. It concludes that 'the UK private healthcare market remains relatively untapped' and is of 'significant interest to US investors'.[25]

The Institute for Healthcare Improvement's National Forum, held in Florida in 2014, saw the attendance of so many high-level staff from NHS Scotland that organizers dubbed their presence Team Scotland. They included Jason Leitch (National Clinical Director Healthcare Quality) and Brian Robson (Executive Clinical Director of Healthcare Improvement Scotland). The Massachusetts-based Institute for Healthcare Improvement, founded by Don Berwick, who led Obamacare, receives funding from insurers Kaiser Permanente and Blue Cross Blue Shield. It was awarded millions of pounds in contracts for NHS Scotland the following year, in 2015.[26]

This chapter has already documented how Minnesota's UnitedHealth Group (and others) conspired to deny coverage to millions of Americans. A subsidiary of UnitedHealth, Optum, has already won NHS consultancy contracts. NHS England's chief executive, Simon Stevens, has held various positions at UnitedHealth.[27]

The foundations for the privatization and deregulation of health services in the US were laid during the Nixon administration, with the promotion of Health Maintenance Organizations (HMOs), the most prominent being Kaiser Permanente. In 1971, Nixon's Assistant to the President for Domestic Affairs, John D Ehrlichman, informed the President that negotiations had stalled on introducing a new privatized healthcare system, the HMO. Ehrlichman approached Nixon for a final decision. 'I'm not too keen on any of these damn medical programs', said the President. 'This is a private enterprise,' Ehrlichman assured him. 'Well, that appeals to me,' Nixon replied. Ehrlichman continued to explain: 'All the incentives are toward less medical care because the less care they give 'em [meaning the public] the more money they make', and went on to point out, 'the incentives run the right way'. 'Fine,' said Nixon. This policy of less care and more privatization paved the way for the HMO Act of 1973.[28]

These decisions had real-world impacts. Since the 1970s, the quality and quantity of American healthcare has declined.

Healthcare specialist Evan M Melhado writes that reforms post-1960s 'increasingly left behind public-interest ideals and their underlying extra-market values in favor of organizing and improving healthcare markets', not healthcare itself. Europeans might fight to keep this or a similar model from being exported to their countries. In a pro-Kaiser Permanente (KP) spiel, the BBC's health correspondent Adam Brimelow revealed that KP advisers were consulting with NHS managers on efficiency and 'new approaches to healthcare'.[29]

The *British Medical Journal* (BMJ) states that the California-based KP has been 'organized so that all doctors from primary, secondary and tertiary care share the budget and responsibility for all care'. In other words, the restructuring of the NHS was a major step towards its Americanization. 'Focusing on minimizing hospital stays', and 'teaching patients how to care for themselves', KP integrates 'funding with provision of service'. Part of the Conservative government's focus on big data and ICT systems in the NHS is an attempt to foster US-style integration of care. The BMJ explains that the goal is 'to have patients diagnosed and treated in multi-speciality health centres where primary-care teams work, lunch, and socialize with specialty nurses and doctors, laboratory and imaging technicians, and with the pharmacy team'. We can assume that choices related to patient care will be dependent on affordability, as in the US. 'Recently, this arrangement has been further integrated by a shared electronic data system,' the journal article concludes.[30]

Data protection and ICT in the NHS

The effect of privatization is to make the NHS dysfunctional. Further private consultants, insurers and service providers can then be brought in to clean up the mess.

One of the biggest wastages came with 'care.data'. From 1997 to 2010, the Institute and Faculty of Actuaries acquired 47 million British national insurance holders' data 'in order to help insurance companies "refine" their premiums'. The Institute cross-referenced data with credit-rating agencies (including Experian) which track the health and habits of millions of consumers. The Brookings Institution says that, in comparison to US models, privacy law in France has constrained the insurance market because it limits the amount of patient information shared between providers and insurers. France's administrative costs are low (5 per cent in 2002), compared with the US (14 per cent in the same year). In the US, the large number of persons without health insurance (16 per cent of the population in 2002) puts further strain on the system, with providers raising the cost of insurance for the insured in order to compensate.[31]

Data, communications and intellectual property provisions in FTAs will make it easier for US and domestic insurance companies to access data in France, Britain and elsewhere. Part of the UK government's NHS privatization campaign has been to allow private data-mining firms to find loopholes in privacy laws.

In 1999, Tim Kelsey, a future director of Patients and Information for NHS England, established a private performance-analysis company, Dr Foster. In 2006, 50 per cent of the company was purchased by the NHS Information Centre, a move criticized by the National Audit Office for its use of public money to benefit private companies. In 2013, care. data was launched by the Conservative-Liberal coalition and run by Kelsey, with the aim of centralizing patient records and social data. A report by Cambridge University's *Journal of Technology Science* concludes that 'patient information could be legally shared with stakeholders outside of the NHS or medical research community' – meaning private insurance companies. Yet this chapter has already documented not only the ease with which US insurers access claimants' and patients' records, but also how detrimental that is to the majority of Americans on low incomes.[32]

Although care.data came with an opt-out option, the hundreds of thousands of people who thought they had opted out had not actually done so due to a so-called 'Type 2 (9Nu4)' objection code error. Within 12 months of the scheme's debut, 160 organizations, including 56 private companies, had obtained patient information, including private healthcare providers Bupa, BMI, Care UK and consultants Ernst & Young,

GE Finnamore and McKinsey & Company. So-called data sharing agreements enabled the pharmaceutical companies AstraZeneca, Boots and GlaxoSmithKline access to records until 2015/16. Records were also released to Millman, the UK subsidiary of Reinsurance Group America and to France's reinsurer, Scor.[33]

For decades, private contractors and service providers have been buying NHS contracts. Future 'free trade' agreements are likely not only to make it easier for US companies to provide services for the NHS, but also to make it harder for the UK government (should a genuinely socialist one ever come to power) to extricate itself from these arrangements.

For example, the draft TTIP chapter on 'Cross-border Trade in Services' (Article X.3) states that neither party shall adopt or maintain measures that 'impose limitations on the number of service suppliers whether in the form of numerical quotas, monopolies, exclusive service suppliers, or the requirement of an economic needs test'. The draft TISA 'Annex on Government Procurement' states: 'Each Party shall ensure that the government procurement of services is conducted in a transparent and impartial manner that... ensures that the service market is opened up to competition.'[34]

The digital market is also gaining a stronghold over NHS services. TTIP's 'Electronic Communications/Telecommunications' chapter refers to state regulation and says: 'Each Party shall require their telecommunications regulatory body to... determine after... review whether any such regulation is no longer necessary as the result of meaningful economic competition between providers of such service'. Another Article on Access and Use says: 'Each Party shall ensure that enterprises of the other Party have access to and use of any public telecommunications service, including leased circuits, offered in its territory or across its borders, on reasonable and non-discriminatory terms and conditions.'[35]

The TISA 'Annex on Telecommunications Services' states: 'Each Party shall endeavour to allow full foreign participation in its electronic services, and telecommunications services sectors, through establishment or other means without limitations of foreign capital participation' (square brackets omitted). Another TISA Article states: 'No Party may prevent a supplier of... telecommunications services... and electronic services... from choosing the technologies it desires to use to supply its services subject to requirements necessary to satisfy legitimate public policy interests... provided that any measure restricting such choice is not prepared, adopted, or applied in a manner that creates unnecessary obstacles to trade.'[36]

The New York-based company International Business Machines (IBM) has won an international reputation for computing excellence. IBM has won various contracts with the NHS, notably the Electronic Staff Record (ESR). The ESR provides real-time, self-service functions, such as payroll, eLearning and human resources for 1.4 million employees in England and Wales. Staff using Androids, iOS and PCs will access the ESR as part of the 'Interactive Experience' scheme. 'Targetization' will be incorporated into the database, with the applications sending business intelligence reports and cost-reduction analyses and recommendations to staff. The scheme costs taxpayers around £300 million ($390m).[37]

The Colorado-based Spectralink argues that care time is taken away from patients by nurses who are not using mobile devices. Their solution is the Bring Your Own Device (BYOD) concept, which will supposedly keep staff in the technological loop at all times. Spectralink hopes to crack the British market with devices that set targets, and send alarms, critical notes and more, direct to handsets. If a US company sold the British public its goods (like BYOD) via domestic privatization arrangements and then took tariff-free profits under FTA or BIT rules, it would be hard to understand how this would in any way amount to 'trade'. The California-based Polycom company won contracts to supply the Telestroke Network Project to NHS hospitals. As part of the services, remote stroke victims who, thanks to cuts would otherwise have to wait for consultations, now receive them digitally. The service also provides HD video and audio sharing at five NHS hospitals, where two mobile carts work in sync with physicians' laptops.[38]

Finally, Google's London-based DeepMind project was given access to 1.6 million patients' data in three hospitals (Barnet, Chase Farm and Royal Free), all run under the Royal Free NHS

Trust. The objective was to provide staff with information via apps, called Streams, on patients with kidney disease. However, it was revealed by the *New Scientist* that patients who had had abortions, drug overdoses and HIV were also included on the app. As well as accident and emergency statistics, the Stream app provides data on who visits hospitals and when and for how long. DeepMind appears to be committed to designing a program that can predict if a patient is at risk of developing an illness. There is a growing culture of runaway digitalization and unaccountability for breaches of privacy.[39]

Pushing back

The people of Europe are fighting a two-pronged assault on their healthcare. The first is from domestic politicians acting on behalf of domestic corporations who want to privatize healthcare in general. Those politicians have to be careful not to move too fast or too blatantly, otherwise they risk becoming unelectable by a public that cherishes free healthcare. The other assault is coming from US corporations, who lobby politicians to push through international 'free trade' deals, be they multilateral or bilateral, with the aim of procuring foreign assets. There needs to be a pan-European push-back against neoliberal policies if free healthcare is to survive.

Conclusion

This book has argued that 'free trade' deals are, in reality, a means of pushing for the further privatization of public resources. Be they 'free trade' deals worked out in neat political unions or in one-to-one partnerships, working people bear the costs. Some of the costs of the US-led, post-War trade and investment order have been analysed in this book. Since the deregulation of the financial sector in the 1970s in particular, the costs have included periodic economic shocks, stagnating and/or declining wages, the offshoring of production and the lowering of environmental standards. As some jobs return home, domestic workers no longer find themselves competing exclusively with foreign workers, but also with robots, both physical and software-based.

Most of these changes have occurred as part of so-called 'liberal internationalism'. But, as this book has argued, the nature of the global economy has changed and US trade and investment policy has changed with it. Both 'liberal internationalism' and 'conservative nationalism' are elite-driven agendas. Examples of liberal internationalism are the Trans-Pacific Partnership and membership of the European Union. Examples of conservative nationalism are the arrangement of bilateral instead of multilateral 'free trade' agreements and alleged sovereignty movements, like Brexit.

If we are interested in helping workers and reversing mass privatization, a third way is required, a *people's* globalization (or 'alter-globalization'), in which human beings can travel freely and integrate into other cultures while empowering themselves through unions and via responsive political representatives.

But how do we achieve the people's globalization that is necessary to survive the calamity of global neoliberalism? TTIP was killed – so far, at least – by a combination of grassroots pressure from the progressive Left (as with the hundreds of thousands of demonstrators in Germany) and the coincidence that the 'trade deal' was not pro-American enough for big business (as with the objections raised by Ford).

We must now be vigilant and apply the same kind of pressures to the US in relation to its TTIP-like bilateral deals, like the US-UK 'free trade' agreement being negotiated in secret. This can be done in a number of ways, all of which overlap:

- Support organizations campaigning for social justice.
- Back leftwing governments. Even the US Democratic Party has some socialistic political representatives, like Bernie Sanders, operating within them. Sanders was as much opposed to the TPP and TTIP as Trump, but for different reasons: while Trump said that those deals weren't pro-business enough, Sanders said they weren't sufficiently pro-human rights. Popular pressure on a Sanders-led Democratic Party, for example, could make the Party even more progressive.
- Vote tactically. Even if the most popular opposition party or representative in your area does not represent your political views, it is important to get the most reactionary party out of government.
- Unionize. At work, college or even in rented accommodation, unions can be joined and/or formed to build grassroots platforms for progressive, grassroots, internationalist agendas. Both North American and European unions issued strong statements against the proposed TTIP and, in doing so, further cemented their common goals and concerns.

These factors will combine to put pressure on existing governments and, if not defeat them, at least push them in a more humane direction.

It is unlikely that an ultra-neoliberal political and economic order – the one in which we now find ourselves – can survive. Such an order attempts not only to brainwash citizens but to trap them in a selfish, competitive environment owned and run by virtual monopolies; in other words, an environment in which it is impossible to win, unless you get lucky or come from a wealthy background.

A finite social structure with limited resources cannot support a system of institutionalized greed. The cracks in the system have already become gaping chasms filled by demagogues like Trump. But ordinary people can and must overcome – and indeed are overcoming – the crude propaganda that seeks to alienate them from their own interests by demonizing progressive movements. With the twin catastrophes of climate change and nuclear war/accident hanging over us, we have few alternatives to serious political engagement.

ENDNOTES

Introduction

1 The White House summary says that the USMCA will open Canada's markets to (what are in reality subsidized) US farm products, reduce the limits of data-storage locations in all three countries and allow US biotech companies to withhold drugs from markets for up to 10 years. White House, 'President Donald J Trump Secures A Modern, Rebalanced Trade Agreement with Canada and Mexico', Fact Sheet, 1 Oct 2018, nin.tl/USMCA

2 In July, Trump met with EU representatives to discuss, among other things, 'Reforming the World Trade Organization (WTO) and addressing unfair trade practices'. White House, 'President Donald J Trump Launches a New Reciprocal Trade Relationship with the European Union', 27 July 2018, nin.tl/TrumpEU

3 The Trump administration's annual report to Congress notes that 'the United States erred in supporting China's entry into the WTO on terms that have proven to be ineffective in securing China's embrace of an open, market-orientated trade regime... It is now clear that the WTO rules are not sufficient to constrain China's market-distorting behavior.' Quoted in Lesley Wroughton, 'Trump administration says US mistakenly backed China WTO accession in 2001', Reuters, 19 Jan 2018, nin.tl/TrumponChina

4 Two international-relations professors divide NAFTA-China relations into two phases: 1994-2000 and 2000+. Since Phase Two, 'NAFTA has been deteriorating in terms of trade, investment and intra-industry trade, among other variables, and both Mexico and the United States have been losing ground to third countries such as China'. Enrique Dussel Peters & Kevin P Gallagher, 'NAFTA's uninvited guest', *CEPAL Review*, 2013, 110: 105. In addition, a report for the European Trade Study Group (ETSG) notes that, by the mid-2000s, Mexico was losing its US market share to Chinese products, including computer hardware. Susana Iranzo and Alyson C Ma, 'The Effect of China on Mexico-U.S. Trade: Undoing NAFTA?' ETSG Research Paper, no date, nin.tl/ChinaMexico

5 A few years ago, World Bank President Dr Jim Yong Kim stated: 'Research based on World Bank data has predicted that the proportion of jobs threatened by automation in India is 69 per cent, 77 per cent in China and as high as 85 per cent in Ethiopia.' Jim Yong Kim, 'The World Bank Group's Mission: To End Extreme Poverty', World Bank, 3 Oct 2016, nin.tl/JimYongKim

Taiwan's Foxconn makes iPhones in China for the US giant, Apple. In 2015, it announced plans to automate 30 per cent of its workforce by 2020. In 2016, it announced that 60,000 jobs had already been automated, as well as announcing a three-phase plan to replace workers with automata, or Foxbots. Nick Start, 'iPhone manufacturer Foxconn plans to replace almost every human worker with robots', *The Verge*, 30 Dec 2016, nin.tl/Foxconn

In 2018, it was reported that a Foxconn subsidiary had started replacing what could amount to one in five workers in its Innolux company, which makes LCD panels. James Crabtree, 'Robots threaten Asian jobs', *Nikkei Asian Review*, 6 Apr 2018, nin.tl/robots

1 Free trade: From World War Two to the World Trade Organization

1 On the issue of post-War sovereignty, Winston Churchill, for example, said: 'Neither the sure prevention of war, nor the continuous rise of world organisation will be gained without what I have called the fraternal association of the English-speaking peoples.' 'The Sinews of Power', 5 Mar, 1946, The Churchill Society, London nin.tl/Churchill
The US State Department explains that the US government wanted to establish a United Nations to replace the League of Nations because the latter had failed to stop the rise of Nazi Germany and Japan's invasion of Manchuria. Notice that the US does not include its own invasion of the Philippines among these atrocities. US Department of State, 'The United States and the Founding of the United Nations, Aug 1941– Oct 1945', Office of the Historian and Bureau of Public Affairs, no date, nin.tl/StateDept

2 Federal Reserve quoted in DA Irwin, PC Mavroidis and AO Sykes, *Genesis of the GATT*, Cambridge University Press, 2008.
Harold James's thorough history of the Bretton Woods system is premised on the idea that the 'most persistent problem facing monetary policymakers has been the spillover of potentially damaging effects from the outside world' (p 1). In other words, these institutions act in one sense as a sponge to absorb other countries' procedures, and in another sense they act as a barrier to countries wanting to trade using sovereign instruments, such as national price controls and tariffs.
Because Britain continued to trade in its colonial 'bloc', it was reluctant to lift controls on currency convertibility. Egypt and India had dollar deficits and wanted to continue trading in sterling. Churchill believed that India owed Britain a debt for its military 'protection' in World War Two. India, of course, rejected this, arguing that the sterling exchange rate was forced on India in the first place. James quotes the official British position on the International Monetary Fund, that 'adherence to the IMF must not entail any obligations which would damage the essentials of the sterling area system'. The uncertainty of the experiment didn't diminish the fact that the overall intention was to 'encourage a greater volume of British and European exports, enabl[ing] these countries to earn dollars, and thus help to close the "dollar gap"' (pp 90-1). H James, *International Monetary Cooperation Since Bretton Woods*, International Monetary Fund and Oxford University Press 1996.

3 Office of the Historian, 'The Chinese Revolution of 1949', State Department (US), history.state.gov/milestones/1945-1952/chinese-rev

4 R Vernon, 'The US Government at Bretton Woods and GATT' in O Kirshner (ed), *The Bretton Woods-GATT System*, Routledge, 2015, pp 59-62.

5 Ibid.

6   Irwin et al, op cit.
7   Ibid.
8   Ibid.
9   Ibid.
10 Ibid.
11 R Ossa, 'A "New Trade" Theory of GATT/WTO Negotiations', *Journal of Political Economy*, 119(1), Feb 2011, pp 122-152; International Trade Organization (Interim Commission), *International Organization*, 3(4), Nov 1949, pp 718-720.
12 Irwin et al, op cit.
13 KJ Vandevelde, *Bilateral Investment Treaties: History, Policy, and Interpretation*, Oxford University Press, 2010.
14 Ibid.
15 Ibid.
16 AK Rose, 'Do We Really Know That The WTO Increases Trade?', *The American Economic Review*, 94(1), Mar, 2004, pp 98-114.
17 W Sachs, 'The New US Bilateral Investment Treaties', *Berkeley Journal of International Law*, 2(1), 1984, pp 192-224.
18 D Campbell, 'NHS funding is falling behind European neighbours' average, research finds', *Guardian*, 20 Jan 2016, nin.tl/NHSfundinglag
19 Sachs, op cit.
20 Ibid.
21 Office of the US Trade Representative, 'Bilateral Investment Treaties', no date. ustr.gov/trade-agreements/bilateral-investment-treaties
22 Ibid.
23 Ibid.
24 K Hollington, *How to Kill*, Arrow Books, 2014, p 53.
25 G Corera, 'MI6 and the death of Patrice Lumumba', BBC News Online, 2 Apr 2013, bbc.co.uk/news/world-africa-22006446
26 L Pease, 'Midnight in the Congo', *Probe*, 6(3), Mar-Apr 1999. Pease cautions that the information might not be conclusive proof of their involvement, nin.tl/ProbeCongo
27 J Brooke, 'Zaire, a paradigm of mismanagement', *New York Times*, 4 Feb 1987, nin.tl/NYTZaire
28 US State Department, 'Congo, Democratic Republic Of (Kinshasa) Bilateral Investment Treaty', 3 Aug 1984, nin.tl/Congo
29 ITA, 'American Manufacturing & Trading, Inc. v. Republic of Zaire, ICSID Case No. ARB/93/1', italaw.com/cases/76
30 For example; EE Barry, *Nationalisation in British Politics: The Historical Background*, Stanford University Press, 1965; R Kelf-Cohen, *British Nationalisation: 1945-1973*, Palgrave Macmillan, 1973.
    On media exaggerations of the pitfalls of socialism and the consequent construction of national myths, see J Medhurst, *That Option No Longer Exists: Britain 1974-76*, Zero Books, 2015; T Martin Lopez, *The Winter of Discontent: Myth, Memory, and History*, Liverpool University Press, 2014.
    See also my book *The Great Brexit Swindle*, Clairview Books, 2016, pp 25-26, note 125.

31 M Clarke, *British External Policy-making in the 1990s*, Macmillan, 1992.
32 RE Bohrer and AC Tan, 'Left Turn in Europe? Reactions to Austerity and the EMU', *Political Research Quarterly*, 53(3), Sep 2000, pp 575-595.
33 Ibid.
34 Ibid.
35 CA Hills, 'NAFTA's Economic Upsides: The View from the United States', *Foreign Affairs*, Jan-Feb 2014, 93(1), pp 122-27.
36 DA Irwin, 'The truth about trade', *Foreign Affairs*, July-Aug 2016; S Polaski, 'Mexican Employment, Productivity and Income a Decade after NAFTA', *Carnegie Endowment*, 25 Feb 2004, nin.tl/MexicoNAFTA
37 JG Castañeda, 'NAFTA's Mixed Record: The View from Mexico', *Foreign Affairs*, Jan-Feb2014, 93(1), pp 134-41; V Dropsy, 'NAFTA and the Mexican Economic Crisis: Causality or Coincidence?', *The Social Science Journal*, 1995, 32(4), pp 361-373.
38 Ibid.
39 Polaski, op cit; A Waldkirch, 'The effects of foreign direct investment in Mexico since NAFTA', *The World Economy*, 2010, doi: 10.1111/j.1467-9701.2009.01244.x, pp 710-45; TM Anandan, 'Mexico, Land of Automatización Opportunity'. Robotic Industries Association, 22 Apr 2016, nin.tl/robotics
    Anandan writes: 'Mexico's industrial landscape is on fire, and spreading. From automotive and aerospace, to consumer electronics and the medical device market, Mexico's manufacturing sector is a hotbed for foreign direct investment (FDI). Its nearest NAFTA partner is leading the pack, with the US accounting for 53 per cent of Mexico's $28 billion FDI in 2015'. In a section called 'Free Trade Abounds', Anandan writes that, 'in addition to a skilled, lower-cost workforce, Mexico has some of the most liberal trade policies in the world'.
    On US businesses outperforming UK companies, Waldkirch writes: 'US MNEs [multination enterprises] operating in the United Kingdom are not just more productive than either purely domestic or UK MNEs, but also than foreign firms from other countries operating in the UK.' The largest US firms in Britain – Walmart (ASDA), Amazon, Facebook, Starbucks, Apple, McDonald's and Google – have a large workforce (ie low wages), low-tax regime, poor workers' rights (zero-hours contracts), and source domestically (from the US). Also, US companies operating with FDI tend to be technologically superior to domestic companies.
    On tax avoidance, Margaret Hodge, Chair of the Committee of Public Accounts, said in 2012: 'Amazon, Starbucks, Google, Apple, Asda, Facebook, eBay, IKEA, Intel, Kraft, Coca-Cola – this is not an individual company; this is a generic problem.' House of Commons Committee of Public Accounts, 'HM Revenue and Customs: Annual Report and Accounts', 2011-12: Nineteenth Report of Session 2012-13, HC 716, 3 Dec 2012, p EV 10, nin.tl/taxavoidance
40 Waldkirch, op cit.
41 S Morris & J Passé-Smith, 'What a Difference a Crisis Makes: NAFTA, Mexico, and the United States', *Latin American Perspectives*, May 2001, 28(3), pp 124-149.

42 Ibid.

43 S Anderson & J Cavanagh, 'Happily Ever NAFTA?', *Foreign Policy*, 9 Nov 2009, nin.tl/happilyNAFTA

44 Ibid.

45 Polaski, op cit.

46 M Vander Stichele, 'Chapter 6: Trade in financial service', *The Financial Sector*, Mar 2004, WTO. Vander Stichele is Senior Researcher at the Centre for Research on Multinational Corporations in Amsterdam. Stichele's chapter in a study for the WTO notes that GATS 'is the only agreement at the international level which regulates and liberalizes trade in financial services as well as investment of financial services providers'. GATS applied to 'all' WTO members. Stichele notes that 'Liberalization of financial services is also dealt with in many regional and bilateral trade agreements'. GATS enhances the globalization of private interests. In mode 1, it allows financial firms to provide services to foreign nationals (cross-border trade). In mode 2, it allows foreigners to take out loans (service consumption). Mode 3 allows foreign banks to buy up domestic ones (corporate service provider). Finally, mode 4 allows the cross-border movement of persons.

GATS is one of the many tools in the arsenal for chipping away at government and state authority. Stichele notes that 'many barriers to trade in services and limitations on the operation of foreign services' firms come from government regulations, measures and administrative decisions'. Through bilateral negotiations, signatories adopt a schedule (Most-Favoured Nation [MFN] principle).

See also: K Alexander, 'The GATS and Financial Services: Liberalisation and Regulation in Global Financial Markets' in K Alexander & M Andenas (eds), *The World Trade Organization and Trade in Services*, Martinus Nijhoff, 2008, p 573; RJ Ahearn & IF Fergusson, 'World Trade Organization (WTO): Issues in the Debate on Continued U.S. Participation', Congressional Research Service, 16 June, 2010, p 7.

47 Ahearn & Fergusson, op cit.

48 G Shaffer, J Nedumpara & A Sinha, 'State transformation and the role of lawyers: The WTO, India and transnational legal ordering', *Law and Society Review*, 49(3), 2015, pp 595-629.

49 Ibid.

50 Mandelson quoted in MN Jovanovic, (2nd ed), *The Economics of European Integration*, Edward Elgar Publishing, 2013, p 602.

2 Free trade: the Bush and Obama years

1 PF Cowhey & JD Aronson, 'A new trade order', *Foreign Affairs*, Jan-Feb 1992.

2 Ibid.

3 Ibid.

4 Ibid.

5 B Reich, *Securing the Covenant: United States-Israel Relations After the Cold War*, Praeger, 1995, pp 93-98.

6 Ibid.

7   H Rosen, 'Free Trade Agreements as Foreign Policy Tools: The US-Israel and US-Jordan FTAs' in JJ Schott (ed), *Free Trade Agreements: US Strategies and Priorities*, Institute for International Economics, 2003, pp 51-75.

8   C-SPAN, 'North American Free Trade Agreement Signing', 7 Oct 1992, nin.tl/NAFTAsigning

9   H Clinton, *Living History*, Simon & Schuster, 2004, p 182.

10 L Cardemil, JC Di Tata, and F Frantischek, 'Central America: Adjustment and Reforms in the 1990s', *Finance and Development*, Mar 2000, 7(1), nin.tl/Cardemil

11 JL Flora & E Torres-Rivas (eds), *Central America: 'Developing Societies'*, Macmillan Education, 1989, pp 76-78.

12 Lord Chitnis, 'El Salvador: Military Equipment Sales', House of Lords Deb 8 Dec 1977 vol 387 cc1746-9, nin.tl/Salvadormilitary
    UK Parliament, 'El Salvador', House of Commons Deb 11 Mar 1985 vol 75 c53W, nin.tl/Hansard3Nov85

13 J Corbyn, 'Central America', House of Commons Deb 24 Mar 1987 vol 113 cc319-40, nin.tl/Hansard24Mar1987

14 P Miller, 'How the British Army Cooperated with the Murderous Guatemalan Regime', *Vice*, 31 May 2016, nin.tl/ViceGuatemala

15 Ibid.

16 D Melrose, 'The Threat of a Good Example?', Oxfam, 1989.

17 Center for Justice and Accountability, 'Honduras: Battalion 316: Torture and Forced Disappearance', cja.org/where-we-work/honduras/

18 Office of the US Trade Representative, 'CAFTA-DR (Dominican Republic-Central America FTA)', no date, nin.tl/USTradeRep

19 Ibid.

20 In addition, markets grew in Brazil, China and Indonesia. The value of clothing climbed in Brazil, India and Indonesia by 100 per cent from 2005 to 2009 and declined in Europe, the US and UK (by 63 per cent in the case of the latter). Clothing and footwear companies tend to outsource to small- and medium-sized local producers, says the International Labour Organization. International Labour Organization, 'Wages and Working Hours in the Textiles, Clothing, Leather and Footwear Industries', GDFTCLI/2014, nin.tl/ILOtextiles

21 Office of the US Trade Representative, op cit.

22 C Arceneaux, *Democratic Latin America*, Routledge, 2016, p 83.

23 K Isbester, 'Democracy in Latin America: A Political History' in Isbester (ed), *The Paradox of Democracy in Latin America*, University of Toronto Press, 2011, pp 65-66.

24 J Briceño-Ruiz & I Morales, 'Conclusion' in J Briceño-Ruiz and I Morales (eds), *Post-Hegemonic Regionalism in the Americas*, Routledge, 2017, eBook, nin.tl/post-hegemonic

25 H Clinton, *Hard Choices*, New York, Simon & Schuster, 2014, p 222.

26 Roverto Barra, COPINH, Civic Council of Popular and Indigenous Organizations of Honduras, 25 years of struggle and revolution, 22 Mar 2018, copinhenglish.blogspot.co.uk

27 N Kristof, 'Obama's Death Sentence for Young Refugees', *New York Times*, 25 June 2016, nin.tl/refugeedeathsentence

28 *Democracy Now!*, 'Hear Hillary Clinton Defend Her Role in Honduras Coup When Questioned by Juan González', 13 Apr 2013, nin.tl/Hillary

29 See my book *Britain's Secret Wars*, Clairview Books, 2016.

30 B Obama, 'Statement by the President on the Trans-Pacific Partnership', White House, Office of the Press Secretary, 5 Oct 2015, nin.tl/ObamaTPP

31 C Woodcock, 'Environmental groups push back against the TPP', *Boulder Weekly*, 7 July 2016, nin.tl/TPPecoimpact

32 American Federation of Labor and Congress of Industrial Organizations – AFL-CIO, 'Trans-Pacific Partnership', no date, nin.tl/AFL-CIOTPP

33 Center for Responsive Politics, 'Issue Lookup (TPP)', no date, nin.tl/opensecrets

34 B Obama, 'Remarks by the President on Trade', 8 May 2015, White House, Office of the Press Secretary, nin.tl/Obamaontrade

35 J Tapper, '45 times Secretary Clinton pushed the trade bill she now opposes', CNN, 15 June 2015, nin.tl/Clintonflipflop

36 Clinton, *Hard Choices*, op cit, pp 68-70

37 AMCHAM EU et al., Letter to Mr Karel De Gucht and Mr Michael Froman, 16 Nov 2011, nin.tl/businesseurope

38 European Commission, 'Online public consultation on investment protection and investor-to-State dispute settlement (ISDS) in the Transatlantic Trade and Investment Partnership Agreement (TTIP)', SWD(2015) 3 final, 13 Jan 2015, nin.tl/TTIPconsultation; White House Office of the Press Secretary, 'Remarks... on the Transatlantic Trade and Investment Partnership', 17 June 2013, nin.tl/TTIPremarks

On the UK's record of turning away needy asylum seekers, Home Office data reveal that: 'The largest increase' in removals of asylum seekers by the British border authorities in 2015, 'compared with the previous year was for Iraqi nationals (+702; +949%) followed by Syrian nationals (+455; +183%)'. Home Office, 'National Statistics: Removals and voluntary departures', 3 Mar 2016, nin.tl/removals

For a breakdown of student, worker and family-related immigrants see: Office for National Statistics, 'Statistical bulletin: Migration Statistics Quarterly Report: May 2016', nin.tl/ONSstats

Refugees and migrants also face violence in Europe. See Amnesty International's documentation of excessive force and arbitrary detention: Policing Demonstrations in the European Union' Oct 2012, amnesty.org.uk/sites/default/files/eu-police.pdf

39 AMCHAM EU et al, op cit, nin.tl/businesseurope

40 nin.tl/ObamaCameron

41 Confederation of British Industry, 'Taking EU-US trade to the next level – why Europe needs TTIP', CBI Briefing, 2015, nin.tl/CBI

42 Confederation of British Industry, 'Business priorities for growing UK exports', CBI Exports Briefing 2015, nin.tl/CBIexports

3 Free trade: The Trump years

1 D Trump and D Shiflett, *The America We Deserve*, Renaissance Books, 2000, pp 145, 146.

2 D Trump, *Time to Get Tough: Making America #1 Again*, Regnery, 2011.

3   D Trump, *Great Again: How to Fix Our Crippled America,* Threshold
    Editions-Simon & Schuster, 2016, pp 86-87.
4   For an overview of the thinking around these trade agreements:
    R Berman, 'Republicans Sour on Obama's Trade Pact', *The Atlantic,* 5 Oct
    2015, nin.tl/RepublicansSour
        DJ Ikenson, 'Currency Manipulation and the Trans-Pacific Partnership',
    Cato Institute, 26 Jan 2015, nin.tl/TPPcurrency
        Value Added Tax (US), 'TPP – Competitive Disadvantage(s)', 20 Oct 2015,
    vatinfo.org/tag/trans-pacific-partnership
        R Goulder, 'Diagnosis: Donald Trump Suffers From VAT Envy', *Forbes,*
    21 Dec 2016, nin.tl/Forbestax
        Alan Tonelson, 'Opinion: Pacific trade deal won't close massive tax
    loophole that kills American jobs', MarketWatch, 31 Mar 2015, nin.tl/
    marketwatch
        C Freund, 'Trump Is Right: 'Border Adjustment' Tax Is Complicated',
    Bloomberg, 18 Jan 2017, nin.tl/Bloombergtax
        B Jopson, 'Corporate America lobbies Trump for tax reversal', *Financial
    Times,* 28 Nov 2016, nin.tl/taxreversal (behind paywall)
        R Teague Beckwith, 'Carl Icahn to Spend $150 Million on Corporate Tax
    Reform', *TIME,* 21 Oct 2015, nin.tl/Icahn
        C Icahn, 'Letter Discussing Desperately Needed Legislation', 21 Oct
    2015, nin.tl/Icahn2
        J Urry, *Offshoring,* Polity Press, 2014.
        E Morphy, 'AT Kearney Predicts The End Of Offshoring As We Know It',
    Forbes, 11 Jan 2016, nin.tl/offshoringend
        D Trump, 'Transcript: President Donald Trump's rally in Melbourne,
    Florida', *Vox,* 18 Feb 2017, nin.tl/Trumprally
        The Economist, 'On the turn', 19 Jan 2013, nin.tl/Indiaturn
        K Flinders, 'IBM India staff reductions are sign of shift in outsourcing
    sector', *Computer Weekly,* no date, nin.tl/Indiajoblosses
        IF Fergusson, MA McMinimy & BR. Williams, 'The Trans-Pacific
    Partnership (TPP) Negotiations and Issues or Congress', Congressional
    Research Service, 20 Mar 2015,
        fas.org/sgp/crs/row/R42694.pdf
        J Calmes, 'Trans-Pacific Partnership Is Reached, but Faces Scrutiny in
    Congress',
        New York Times, 5 Oct 2015, nin.tl/TPPscrutiny
        A Behsudi, 'Hatch wants TPp and his 12 years, too', *Politico,* 28 Sep
    2016, nin.tl/PoliticoTPp
5   JI Domínguez and RF de Castro, 'US-Mexico Relations: Coping with
    Domestic and International Crises' in Domínguez and de Castro (eds.),
    *Contemporary U.S.-Latin American Relations: Cooperation or Conflict in the
    21st Century?* (2nd ed), Routledge, 2016.
6   World Trade Organization, 'United States countervailing measures on
    certain hot-rolled carbon steel flat products from India', Report of the
    Panel, WT/DS436/R, 14 July 2014, nin.tl/Hatch
        World Trade Organization, 'India files dispute against the US over
    non-immigrant temporary working visas', 4 Mar 2016, nin.tl/Indiafiles

World Trade Organization, 'DS437: United States–Countervailing Duty Measures on Certain Products from China', 21 July 2016, nin.tl/WTOdisputes

7 Young Jong Choi, 'A rise of regionalist ideas in East Asia' in J Dominguez and Byung Kook Kim (eds), *Between Compliance and Conflict*, Routledge, 2005, p 69, nin.tl/TPPscrutiny

C Dent, 'Free Trade Agreements in the Asia-Pacific'', The Evian Group, Policy Brief, Apr 2006.

P Lamy, 'Regional agreements: the "pepper" in the multilateral "curry"', WTO, 17 Jan 2007, nin.tl/pepper

8 Standard BIT template. BITs are available at US State Department, 'Bilateral Investment Treaties and Related Agreements', no date, nin.tl/BIT

9 Almost the same wording made its way into CAFTA, indicating the cut-and-paste nature of bi- and multilateral deals. This should serve as a warning to activists: that Trump's apparent nationalism and bilateralism is no better than multilateralism. See CAFTA, Chapter 16 Labor, Article 16.2(B), Enforcement of Labor Laws, nin.tl/CAFTA

10 US State Department, '2012 U.S. Model Bilateral Investment Treaty'. state.gov/documents/organization/188371.pdf

11 S Woolcock, 'European Union policy towards Free Trade Agreements', ECIPE, Working Paper 03/2007, Dec 2014, nin.tl/EUpolicy

12 Ibid.

13 D Yilmazkuday & H Yilmazkuday, 'Bilateral versus Multilateral Free Trade Agreements: A Welfare Analysis', *Review of International Economics*, 2014, 22(3), pp 513–535, nin.tl/MultiversusBi

14 Ibid.

15 D Trump, 'Presidential Memorandum Regarding Withdrawal of the United States from the Trans-Pacific Partnership Negotiations and Agreement', White House Office of the Press Secretary, 23 Jan 2017, nin.tl/WhiteHousewithdraws

16 J Trudeau, 'Joint Statement from President Donald J Trump and Prime Minister Justin Trudeau', 13 Feb 2017, nin.tl/TrumpTrudeau

17 White House Office of the Press Secretary, 'Joint Statement from President Donald J. Trump and Prime Minister Shinzo Abe', 10 Feb 2017, nin.tl/TrumpAbe

18 White House Office of the Press Secretary, 'Readout of the President's Call with Prime Minister Bill English of New Zealand', 5 Feb 2017, nin.tl/TrumpEnglish

19 White House Office of the Press Secretary, 'Remarks by President Trump and President Pedro Pablo Kuczynski of Peru Before Bilateral Meeting', 24 Feb 2017, nin.tl/TrumpPeru

20 A Fensom, 'While Trump and Abe Eye Bilateral Pact, Australia Keeps TPp Alive', *The Diplomat*, 12 Feb 2017, nin.tl/TPPalive

4 Rivalries: 'Globalization is a brutal process'

1 See my book *Britain's Secret Wars*, Clairview Books, 2016.

2 R Toye, *Churchill's Empire: The World that Made Him and the World He Made*, Macmillan, 2010, p ix.

Mark Curtis, *Unpeople: Britain's Secret Human Rights Abuses*, Vintage, 2004, p 137.

3 Quoted in PJ Cain and M Harrison (eds), *Imperialism: Critical Concepts in Historical Studies, Vol 2*, Routledge, 2001, p 104, note 19.

4 Ibid.

5 Chatham House, 'Globalization and World Order', May 2014, nin.tl/Chatham

6 Ibid.

7 Comprehensive Economic and Trade Agreement (CETA) between Canada and the European Union, nin.tl/CETA

8 C Vidler, 'The Canada-Europe Comprehensive Economic & Trade Agreement (CETA)', Canadian Chamber of Commerce, 3 Mar 2014, nin.tl/CETA2

9 A Gardner, 'Speech: Ambassador Gardner's Remarks at Chatham House on Global Trade', US Mission to the European Union, 11 July 2016, nin.tl/Gardner

10 Ibid.

11 Ibid.

12 See my book *The Great Brexit Swindle*, Clairview, 2016, and *President Trump, Inc*, Clairview, 2017.

13 *President Trump, Inc.* op cit, pp 136-38.

14 Ibid.

15 Suisheng Zhao, 'Chinese Nationalism and Approaches toward East Asian Regional Cooperation', Council on Foreign Relations, Dec 2009.

16 See: US Commercial Service, *Global Edge* [2017], nin.tl/globaledge
    The members include Brunei, Cambodia, Indonesia, Laos, Malaysia, Myanmar, Philippines, Singapore, Thailand and Vietnam.

17 Association of Southeast Asian Nations (ASEAN), asean.org

18 Shanghai Cooperation Organization (SCO), eng.sectsco.org

19 ASEA, op cit

20 Asia-Pacific Economic Cooperation (APEC), 'Annex A: Lima Declaration on FTAAP', 20 Nov 2016, nin.tl/APEC The other signatories to the RCEP are: Australia, Brunei, Cambodia, India, Indonesia, Japan, Laos, Malaysia, Myanmar, New Zealand, Philippines, Singapore, South Korea, Thailand and Vietnam.

21 Bureau of European and Eurasian Affairs, 'VI. Assessments Required by the Silk Road Strategy Act of 1999', US State Department, Jan 2003, nin.tl/State ; US State Department, 'US Support for the New Silk Road', nin.tl/newSilkRoad The former Soviet states involved were Armenia, Azerbaijan, Georgia, Kazakhstan, Kyrgyzstan, Tajikistan, Turkmenistan and Uzbekistan.

22 For praise, see G Das, *India Unbound*, Anchor Books, 2002. For criticism, A Roy, *Listening to Grasshoppers*, Penguin, 2008.

23 J Meltzer, 'Growing the India-U.S. Trade and Investment Relationship', Brookings Institution, 23 Jun 2016, nin.tl/India-UStrade

24 T Madan, 'India's Relations with China: The Good, the Bad and the (Potentially) Ugly', Brookings Institution, 8 Oct 2013,nin.tl/India-UStrade
    R Iyengar, 'India boycotts China's global trade jamboree', CNN Money, 15 May 2017, nin.tl/Indiaboycott
    N Watt, P Lewis & T Branigan, 'US anger at Britain joining Chinese-led

investment bank AIIB', *Guardian*, 13 Mar 2015, nin.tl/USanger

25 D Roy Chaudhury, 'India, Russia plan Free Trade Agreement in Eurasian region', *The Economic Times*, 29 May 2017, nin.tl/India-Russia

26 M Selden, 'A forgotten Holocaust', *Asia-Pacific Journal*, 5(5), May 2007, nin.tl/Selden

27 See TJ Coles, 'US-Japan "Defense" Deal Provokes China, Japanese Public Protest', *Axis of Logic*, 24 July 2015, nin.tl/Axislogic

28 White House, 'Remarks by President Trump and Prime Minister Abe of Japan in Joint Press Conference', Office of the Press Secretary, 10 Feb 2017, nin.tl/TrumpAbe2

29 US Department of State, '2013 Investment Climate Statement – Japan', Bureau of Economic and Business Affairs, Mar 2013, nin.tl/StateonJapan

30 European Commission, 'Trade Sustainability Impact Assessment of the Free Trade Agreement between the European Union and Japan', Directorate-General for Trade, 2016, nin.tl/EUJapan

31 RJ Anderson, 'A History of President Putin's Campaign to Re-Nationalize Industry and the Implications for Russian Reform and Foreign Policy', US Army War College, PA 17013-5050, Aug 2002, nin.tl/Putinimplications

32 M Katusa, 'Vladimir Putin is the new global shah of oil', *Forbes*, 29 Oct 2012, nin.tl/GlobalShah

33 US State Department, 'Ukraine and Russia Sanctions', state.gov/e/eb/tfs/spi/ukrainerussia

34 Y Torbati & E Scheyder, 'Exxon sues US over fine levied for Russia deal under Tillerson', Reuters, 20 July 2017, nin.tl/Exxonsues

5 Activists: 'Get a life!'

1 European Commission Climate Action, '2020 climate and energy package', no date, nin.tl/2020EU
    A Neslen, 'EU set to emit 2bn tonnes more CO_2 than Paris climate pledge', *Guardian*, 29 Feb 2016, nin.tl/2billion

2 A Neslen, 'Wind power generates 140% of Denmark's electricity demand', *Guardian*, 10 July 2015, nin.tl/Denmark_
    Energy Information Administration (US), 'Germany's renewables electricity generation grows in 2015, but coal still dominant', 24 May 2016, nin.tl/EIAGermany
    A Neslen, 'Portugal runs for four days straight on renewable energy alone', *Guardian*, 18 May 2016, nin.tl/Portugal

3 TJ Donohue, 'TTIP: A Transatlantic Business Imperative', US Chamber of Commerce, 7 Apr 2014, nin.tl/TTIPimperative

4 A Little, 'UK government ends onshore wind farm subsidies for good', *Daily Express*, 20 Feb 2016, nin.tl/onshorewind

5 Department of Energy and Climate Change, 'Guidance on fracking: developing shale oil and gas in the UK', 11 Apr 2016, nin.tl/frackingguidance

6 C. Le Quéré et al, 'Global carbon budget 2014', *Earth System Science Data*, Vol 6, 2014, pp 1-90, nin.tl/globalcarbon
    NASA, 'Changes in the Carbon Cycle', no date, nin.tl/NASAoncarbon
    European Commission, 'Welcome to the homepage of EDGAR', edgar.jrc.ec.europa.eu

7 Emissions Database for Global Atmosphere Research, 'Emissions data', European Commission Joint Research Commission, live document, edgar. jrc.ec.europa.eu

8 World Bank, 'Electric power consumption (kWh per capita)', 2014, nin.tl/poweruse
   Food and Agricultural Organization, 'Food Consumption Nutrients', 2006-08, nin.tl/FAO

9 Statista, 'Direct investment position of the United States in China from 2000 to 2014 (in billions of US dollars, on a historical-cost basis)', live document, https://nin.tl/USinChina
   RA McCormack, 'America's Biggest Companies Continue To Move Factories Offshore and Eliminate Thousands of American Jobs', *Manufacturing and Technology News*, 31 July 2010, 20(10). sbeinc.com/resources/cms.cfm?fuseaction=news.detail&articleID=1626&pageID=25

10 United States Environmental Protection Agency (EPA), 'Carbon dioxide emissions', no date, Overview of Greenhouse Gases, nin.tl/offshore
   On the EPA's awful record, consider the following: the EPA declared the air in Manhattan safe to breathe after 9/11, even though its top officials knew the air was toxic. J Walters, 'Former EPA head admits she was wrong to tell New Yorkers post-9/11 air was safe', *Guardian*, 10 Sep 2011. The EPA also acknowledges toxicity in nanotechnology, but advises against a total or partial ban, and also advises against the precautionary principle: EPA, 'Nanotechnology White Paper', EPA 100/B-07/001, Feb 2007, nin.tl/EPAnanotech

11 H Clinton, *It Takes a Village*, New York, Simon & Schuster, 2006, p xvi.

12 H Clinton, *Living History*, New York, Thorndike Press, 2003, pp 249 & 317.

13 Ibid, pp 359-60.

14 Ibid, p 446.

15 Ibid, p 236.

16 H Clinton, *Hard Choices*, New York, Simon & Schuster, 2014.

17 H Clinton, 'Assess the potential for international shale gas development', 29 Oct 2009, nin.tl/wikileakscables

18 Ibid.

19 WikiLeaks, 'S/CIEA Goldwyn visit to Ottawa', 2 Oct 2011, nin.tl/wikileaksOttawa

20 M Blake, 'How Hillary Clinton's State Department Sold Fracking to the World', *Mother Jones*, Sep-Oct 2014, nin.tl/sellingfracking
   L Fang & S Horn, 'Hillary Clinton's energy initiative pressured countries to embrace fracking, new emails reveal', *The Intercept*, 23 May 2016, nin.tl/frackingpressure

21 Blake, op cit.

22 Fang & Horn, op cit.

23 Blake, op cit & M Chiriac, 'Romanian PM changes tack over fracking', *Balkans Insight*, 29 Jan 2013, nin.tl/Romaniafracking

24 Blake, op cit.

25 L Boisson de Chazournes, 'United Nations Framework Convention on Climate Change', United Nations Audiovisual Library of International

Law, 2008. legal.un.org/avl/pdf/ha/ccc/ccc_e.pdf
B Adler, 'Obama has a plan for getting around Senate opposition to a climate treaty', *Grist*, 2 Aug 2014, nin.tl/Adler

26 One of many books on the subject is PR Keefe's *Chatter: Uncovering the Echelon Surveillance Network and the Secret World of Global Eavesdropping*, Random House, 2006.

27 Ibid.

28 S Gjerding, A Geist, H Moltke & L Poitras, 'For the NSA, espionage was a means to strengthen the US position in climate negotiations', *Information*, 30 Jan 2014, nin.tl/NSA

29 Ibid.

30 Ibid.

31 *Guardian*, 'Draft Copenhagen climate change agreement – the "Danish text"', 8 Dec 2009, nin.tl/Copenhagen

32 J Coleman, 'Hillary Clinton's Connections to the Oil and Gas Industry', Greenpeace USA, 21 Apr 2016, nin.tl/GreenpeaceUS

33 Ibid.

34 S Hall, 'Exxon knew about climate change almost 40 years ago', *Scientific American*, 26 Oct 2015, nin.tl/Exxon

35 Coleman, op cit.

36 Ibid.

37 Ibid.

38 Ibid.

39 TransCanada Corporation, 'Notice of intent to submit a claim to arbitration under Chapter 11 of the North American Free Trade Agreement', 6 Jan 2016, nin.tl/KeystoneXL

40 DW Frank, 'Memorandum opinion and order', 2010, nin.tl/Sierra

41 C Cray, 'Fossil Fuel Lobbyists' Contributions to the Clinton Campaign', Greenpeace USA, 22 Apr 2016, nin.tl/GreenpeaceUS2

42 SA Miller, 'Hillary's agribusiness ties give rise to nickname in Iowa: "Bride of Frankenfood"', *Washington Times*, 17 May 2015, nin.tl/Monsantoties

43 USAID, 'USAID Administrator Highlights Private Sector Partnerships to Reduce Hunger and Poverty at the World Economic Forum', Feed the Future, 28 Jan 2011, nin.tl/USAID
J Kerry, 'Message from the Secretary of State' in *Feed the Future, Progress Report*, June 2013, nin.tl/Kerry

44 Kerry, op cit.

45 Feed the Future, 'Making the Most of a Good Thing', 28 Mar 2013, nin.tl/feedfuture

46 Ibid.

47 XiaoZhi Lim, 'Video: Hillary Clinton endorses GMOs, solution-focused crop biotechnology', Genetic Literacy Project, 29 July 2016. nin.tl/GMOs
Biology Innovation Organization, 'Members', no date, bio.org/bio-member-directory

48 C Gillam, 'Big campaign cash for Clinton from Monsanto lobbyist', *Truth-Out*, 6 Feb 2016, nin.tl/Gillam

49 WikiLeaks, 'Transcript, Building Trades Union (Keystone XL).docx', 2016.

wikileaks.org/podesta-emails/emailid/9617
50 K Mathiesen, 'Clinton pulled climate from speeches after Sanders endorsement', Climate Home, 20 Sep 2016, nin.tl/postSanders

6 Fossil fuels: 'Exploitation should be guaranteed'

1 P De Micco, 'Could US oil and gas exports be a game changer for EU energy security?' Directorate General for External Policies, European Parliament, Feb 2016, nin.tl/gamechanger
2 US Energy Information Administration, 'How much petroleum does the United States import and export?', no date, nin.tl/USoilexports
3 Eurostat, 'Energy production and imports', no date, nin.tl/EUoilimports
4 Ibid.
5 Forbes, 'The World's Biggest Oil and Gas Companies', live document, nin.tl/Forbesoil
6 KJ Benes, 'Considerations for the Treatment of Energy in the US-EU Transatlantic Trade and Investment Partnership', Lugar Center, Sep 2015, nin.tl/TTIPenergy
7 Global Energy Institute (US Chamber of Commerce), 'Is US breaking the law by restricting LNG exports?', Platts Inside Energy, no date, nin.tl/LNGexports
8 Eurostat, op cit. No date.
9 European Commission, 'Energy and raw materials in TTIP', nin.tl/TTIPenergy2
   European Commission, 'EU-US Transatlantic Trade and Investment Partnership: Raw materials and energy', July 2013, nin.tl/TTIPenergy3
10 Energy Information Administration (US), 'Oil and gas industry employment growing much faster than total private sector employment', 8 Aug 2013, nin.tl/oilwork
   C Helman, 'The 93 billionaires in global oil and energy', Forbes, 9 Mar 2016, nin.tl/oilbillionaires
   T DiChristopher, 'Oil and gas jobs' pay is still big, but not booming', CNBC, 22 July 2015, nin.tl/oilpay.
   US Department of Labor, 'Oil and gas extraction', Health and Safety Topics, live document, nin.tl/OSHA
11 White House, 'Fact Sheet: President Obama's 21st century clean transportation system', Office of the Press Secretary, 4 Feb 2016, nin.tl/cleantransport
12 C Isidore, 'The Obama oil boom', CCN Money, 28 Jan 2015, nin.tl/Obamaboom
13 EB Scott, 'Chevron Corporation: Comments on Proposed Transatlantic Trade and Investment Partnership', 7 May 2013, letter to Douglas Bell, Chairman, Trade Policy Staff Committee, Office of the US Trade Representative, Docket USTR-2013-0019, nin.tl/ChevronTTIP
14 Center for Responsive Politics, 'Oil and Gas: Industry Profile: Summary, 2016', nin.tl/lobbyoil
   A Pandey, 'US fossil fuel subsidies increase 'dramatically' despite climate change pledge', International Business Times, 12 Nov 2015, nin.tl/oilsubsidies

S Nyquist, 'Lower oil prices but more renewables: What's going on?', *The McKinsey Quarter,* June 2015, nin.tl/renewablesup

15 A Neslen, 'TTIP: Chevron lobbied for controversial legal right as 'environmental deterrent'', *Guardian,* 26 Apr 2016, nin.tl/Chevronlobby

16 Scott, op cit.

17 Ibid.

18 TISA, 'Trade in Services Agreement: Q&A on Proposal for Energy Related Services Annex [draft]', 3 Dec 2015, nin.tl/TISAleak

19 M Morton, 'Is There Still a Role for Oil Companies in Renewables?', *Greentech Media* and *Nexant,* 12 Mar 2015, nin.tl/renewablegrab
   T Randall, 'Fossil fuels just lost the race against renewables', *Bloomberg,*
   14 Apr 2015, nin.tl/renewablesrace

20 International Energy Agency, 'Oil', live document, iea.org/aboutus/faqs/oil/

21 Nyquist, op cit.

22 Ibid.

7 Vehicles: Investor-State dispute settlements as 'gunboat diplomacy'

1 European Commission, 'Transatlantic Trade and Investment Partnership: The Economic Analysis Explained', Sep 2013, nin.tl/TTIPexplained
   Environmental Protection Agency, 'Volkswagen Light Duty Diesel Vehicle Violations for Model Years 2009-2016 Share', live document, epa.gov/vw

2 TISA, 'Annex on Road Freight Transport and Related Logistics Services [draft]', July 2015, nin.tl/TISAannex

3 Ibid.

4 M Evans, 'Britain's "bold" £15 billion road-building plans unveiled – including Stonehenge tunnel', *Express,* 3 Dec 2014, nin.tl/ UKroadbuilding

5 K Corcoran, 'Revealed: How Government "cost the UK BILLIONS" by slashing flood defence budget', *Express,* 29 Dec, 2015, nin.tl/floodbudget
   Department for Transport, Freedom of Information Request, The 'Action for Roads' project (2013), Ref F0011940, 16 Jan 2015.

6 US Chamber of Commerce, 'Top Ten Environmental Myths', 2004, nin.tl/ top10myths
   M Klare, *Blood and Oil: The Dangers and Consequences of America's Growing Petroleum Dependency,* Owl Books, 2004.
   On the connection between oil prices, house prices and the 2008 Crash, see, for example, the blog by Berkeley professor David Zilberman, nin.tl/Zilberman

7 United States Department of Energy, 'The History of the Electric Car', 15 Sep 2014, energy.gov/articles/history-electric-car
   Idaho National Laboratory, 'The History of Electric Cars', Advanced Vehicle Testing Activity, nin.tl/electrichistory

8 FP Miller, AF Vandome and J McBrewster, *Great American Streetcar Scandal,* VDM Publishing, 2010.

J Chu, 'Study: Air pollution causes 200,000 early deaths each year in the U.S.', *MIT News*, 29 Aug 2013, nin.tl/pollutiondeaths

9 R A Jansen, *Second Generation Biofuels and Biomass*, Wiley-VCH, 2012.

J Hirsch, '253 million cars and trucks on US roads', *LA Times*, 9 June 2014, nin.tl/carage

M Ferrazzi, 'The Automotive Industry After the Crisis: Where Does Europe Stand?' in Luciano Ciravenga (ed), *Sustaining Industrial Competitiveness after the Crisis*, Palgrave Macmillan, 2012.

CEN and ESTI (European Committee for Standardisation), 'CEN and ETSI deliver first set of standards for Cooperative Intelligent Transport Systems',, 12 Feb 2014, nin.tl/connectedcars

Union of Concerned Scientists, 'Cars, Trucks, and Air Pollution', UCS, 5 Dec 2014, nin.tl/vehiclepollution

10 European Automobile Manufacturers Association (ACEA), no title, no date, nin.tl/ACEA

11 World Bank, 'Motor vehicles (per 1,000 people)', 2013, nin.tl/cardensity

12 Chu, op cit.

13 WHO, '7 million premature deaths annually linked to air pollution', 25 Mar 2014, nin.tl/WHOair

14 Ibid.

15 Office of the United States Trade Representative, 'Fact Sheet: Investor-State Dispute Settlement (ISDS)', Mar 2015, nin.tl/ISDSfacts

16 Ibid.

17 UNCTAD, 'Recent Trends in IIAS and ISDS', No 1, Feb 2015, nin.tl/UNCTADtrends

European Commission, 'Investor-to-State Dispute Settlement (ISDS): Some facts and figures', 12 Mar 2015, nin.tl/ISDSfacts2

18 European Commission (2015), op cit.

19 European Commission (2015) and UNCTAD, ibid.

20 House of Lords, 'The Transatlantic Trade and Investment', House of Lords European Union Committee, 14th Report of Session 2013-14, nin.tl/LordsTTIP

21 M Barlow, 'Canada is the most sued country in the "developed" world, and that should sound alarm bells in the EU', *Global Justice Now*, 30 Oct 2015. Amounts given in the article are in euros and have been converted to US dollars in the text, nin.tl/Canadamostsued

22 Government of Canada, 'NAFTA Chapter 11 Investment Cases Filed Against the Government of Canada: Lone Pine Resources v. Government of Canada', 22 Mar 2016, nin.tl/LonePine

23 AC Swan, 'Ethyl Corporation v. Canada, Award on Jurisdiction (under NAFTA/UNCITRAL)', *The American Journal of International Law*, 94(1), Jan 2000, pp 159-166.

24 'NAFTA Panel Rules in US Favor in Methanex Case,' *The American Journal of International Law*, vol 99, no 4, 2005, pp 920–921, jstor.org/stable/3396696

25 M Pérez-Rocha, 'When Corporations Sue Governments', *New York Times*, 3 Dec 2014, nin.tl/NYTsuing

26 Ibid.

27 International Centre for Settlement of Investment Disputes, ICSID Case
No. ARB/06/11, 2 Nov 2015, nin.tl/Ecuadorsuit

28 Ibid.

29 Ibid.

30 *Andes*, 'Ecuador cuts 800 million dollar spending and announces fiscal
deficit reduction for next year', 19 Aug 2015, nin.tl/Ecuadorcut

8 Food and agriculture: 'Mere law'

1 World Food Programme, 'Hunger Statistics', live document, wfp.org/
hunger/stats.

United States Department of Agriculture Economic Research Services,
'Global Food Industry', 10 May 2016, nin.tl/USDAglobal

On food market manipulation by banks, see, for instance: MW Masters,
'Testimony of Michael W Masters Managing Member/Portfolio Manager
Masters Capital Management, LLC', Committee on Homeland Security
and Governmental Affairs United States Senate, 20 May 2008. Masters
says: 'The CFTC [Commodity Futures Trading Commission] has granted
Wall Street banks an exemption from speculative position limits when
these banks hedge over-the-counter swaps transactions. This has
effectively opened a loophole for unlimited speculation. When Index
Speculators enter into commodity index swaps, which 85-90% of them
do, they face no speculative position limits.' Masters goes on: 'The
really shocking thing about the Swaps Loophole is that Speculators of
all stripes can use it to access the futures markets. So if a hedge fund
wants a $500-million position in Wheat, which is way beyond position
limits, they can enter into a swap with a Wall Street bank and then the
bank buys $500 million worth of Wheat futures' (p. 7), nin.tl/Masters

See also, T Jones, 'The great hunger lottery: How banking speculation
causes food crises', World Development Movement, July 2010, p7, nin.tl/
hungerlottery

Jones writes: 'From early 2007 to the middle of 2008 there was a huge
spike in food prices. Over the period there was more than an 80-per-cent
increase in the price of wheat on world markets. The price of maize
similarly shot up by almost 90 per cent. Prices then fell rapidly in a
matter of weeks in the second half of 2008. There are various reasons to
explain a general increase in food prices over this time. But only financial
speculation can explain the extent of the wild swings in the price of food.'

2 EC Madu, 'Investment and development will secure the Rights of the
Child', UNICEF, no date, unicef.org/rightsite/364_617.htm

A Taylor & R Loopstra, 'Too poor to eat: Food insecurity in the UK',
Food Foundation UK, May 2016, nin.tl/foodfoundation

J Pan & H Wei (eds), 2015, *Annual Report on Urban Development of
China 2013*, Springer, p 7.

JF Reid, 'The Impact of Mechanization on Agriculture', *The Bridge on
Agriculture and Information Technology*, 41(3), nin.tl/Reid

On the issue of mechanization in US agribusiness, Reid describes
'agricultural mechanization' as 'one of the great achievements of the 20th
century'. It 'was enabled by technologies that created value in agricultural

production practices through the more efficient use of labor'.

3 S Ross, 'The 4 countries that produce the most food', Investopedia, 6 Oct 2015, nin.tl/Investopedia
    United States Department of Agriculture, Economic Research Service, 'Ag and Food Sectors and the Economy', no date, nin.tl/Agfood
        Statista, 'US Agriculture – Statistics & Facts', nin.tl/Agstats
        FAO, 'FAOSTAT Domains', Statistics Divisions, nin.tl/FAOstats

4 MarketsandMarkets, 'Seeds Market worth $85.2 Billion by 2018', 2016, marketsandmarkets.com/PressReleases/seeds.asp

5 DJ Lynch & A Bjerga, 'Taxpayers turn US farmers into fat cats with subsidies', *Bloomberg*, 9 Sep 2013, nin.tl/fatcats

6 United States Department of Agriculture, 'EU Agricultural Exports, Trade Surplus with U.S. Reach Record Levels in 2015', 31 Mar 2016, nin.tl/EU-USrecord

7 Ibid.

8 Ibid.

9 Corporate Europe Observatory, 'Who lobbies most on TTIP?', 8 July 2014, nin.tl/wholobbiesmost

10 Europe Corporate Observatory, 'FW: Meeting with US and EU seed trade associations', Ref. Ares (2014) 3935988 – 25 11/2014, Mar 2014, nin.tl/seedtrade

11 TTIP, 'Agriculture [US: Market Access] Consolidated Proposals [draft]', no date.
    ttip-leaks.org/patroklos/doc2.pdf

12 Ibid.

13 TPP, 'Chapter 2: National Treatment and Market Access for Goods', 2016, nin.tl/TPPch2.

14 GATT, XIII. Article. XI.A(1), 'General Elimination of Quantitative Restriction', 1994, nin.tl/GATTXIII
    On the Philippines, consider the following: 'US-based biotechnology companies Dow AgriSciences [sic] and Monsanto are now [2005 data] eyeing markets for more potent and pest-resistant GM corn after having successfully marketed the *Bacillus thuringiensis* (Bt) corn since 2003. Bt corn has the sole trait of being Asiatic corn-borer resistant'. The article says: 'Before even setting foot in other Asian countries, biotechnology companies have already seen opportunities in starting out in the Philippines. The country is internationally recognized for having a more established regulatory policy on biotechnology' – meaning it has lax rules on testing and marketing. 'In 2005, Dow AgroSciences has already started its field testing of the 'TC 1507,' in Isabela, South Cotabato, General Santos, and Bukidnon. Branded Herculex in the US, TC 1507 is said to have achieved a good yield advantage of 99.7 percent over non-Bt corn'. Source: ABS-CBN, 'US biotech firms target enhanced GM corn', 4 Nov, 2008, nin.tl/ABS-CBN

15 Agence France-Presse, 'India, US reach breakthrough in row over key WTO pact', 13 Nov 2013.
    M Davis, *Late Victorian Holocausts*, Verso, 2002.

16 ASTA & ESA, 'Transatlantic Trade and Investment Partnership

Agreement (TTIP) Priority Issues for the Seed Sector', Ref. Ares (2015) 2562864 – 18/06/2015, nin.tl/ASTA-ESA

17 TTIP, 'Sanitary and Phytosanitary Measures', no date, nin.tl/TTIPsanitary

18 Ibid.

19 European Commission, 'Pesticides in TTIP', Feb 2015, nin.tl/ TTIPpesticides

20 M Ferreira Maia and SJ Moore, 'Plant-based insect repellents', *Malaria Journal*, 2011, Vol 10, doi: 10.1186/1475-2875-10-S1-S11, nin.tl/malaria

21 W Biddle, 'Nerve gases and pesticides', *New York Times*, 30 Mar 1984, nin.tl/nervegas
On Colombia, see my *Britain's Secret Wars*, Clairview Books, 2016, pp 115-17.

22 PAN, 'Pesticides and health hazards: Facts and figures', 2012. pan-germany.org/download/Vergift_EN-201112-web.pdf

23 Ibid.

24 MP Walls &BP Glenn, 'Consideration of Endocrine Disruptors in the EU', American Chemistry Council and CropLife America, letter to Mr Jim Jones, Office of Chemical Safety and Pollution Prevention, 3 Dec 2012, nin.tl/endocrine

25 A Neslen, 'Health costs of hormone disrupting chemicals over €150bn a year in Europe, says study', *Guardian*, 6 Mar 2015, nin.tl/HDCs

26 S Horel, 'A Toxic Affair', Corporate Europe Observatory, 19 May 2015, nin.tl/toxic
A Kortenkamp et al, 'State of the art assessment of endocrine disrupters', Contract No. 070307/2009/550687/SER/D3, 23 Dec, 2011, nin.tl/EDC2
Corporate Europe Observatory, 'EFSA used to defend industry in lobbying battle on chemicals?', 12 Dec 2012, nin.tl/EFSA
European Centre for Ecotoxicology and Toxicology of Chemicals, 'Workshop on Risk Assessment of Endocrine Disrupting Chemicals', 9-10 May 2011, Florence, nin.tl/EDC3

27 Horel, op cit
Å Bergman et al, 'State of the Science of Endocrine Disrupting Chemicals – 2012', WHO& UNEP, 2013, nin.tl/EDCUNEP
T Spence, 'MEP calls for parliamentary risk panel to tame green 'scaremongering', nin.tl/euractiv
Scientific Opinion on the hazard assessment of endocrine disruptors, European Food Safety Authority, 2013, nin.tl/EDC4

28 Horel, op. cit.

29 Statista, 'Acreage of genetically modified crops worldwide from 2004 to 2015, by leading country (in million hectares)', no date, nin.tl/GMOglobal

30 Christen Brownlee, 'Biography of Rudolf Jaenisch', PNAS, 101(39), pp 13982-84. Genetech, 'First successful laboratory production of human insulin announced', 6 Sep 1978, nin.tl/genetech
RM Skivin, 'The use of genetically engineered bacteria to control frost on strawberries and potatoes', *Scientia Horticulturae*, 84(1-2), Apr 2000, pp 179-189.

31 EUROPA, 'Council Directive 90/220/EEC of 23 Apr 1990 on the deliberate

release into the environment of genetically modified organisms', nin.tl/
GMOEuropa

32 R Johnson, 'The US-EU Beef Hormone Dispute', Congressional Research
Service, 14 Jan 2015, nin.tl/beefhormones

33 H Stein, 'Intellectual Property and Genetically Modified Seeds',
Northwestern Journal of Technology and Intellectual Property, 3(2), Spring,
2005, nin.tl/IPGMOs
    K Bustos, 'Sowing the Seeds of Reason in the Field of the Terminator
Debate', *Journal of Business Ethics*, 77(1), Jan 2008, pp 65-72.

34 N Assinder, 'Blair backs modified food', 15 Feb 1999, nin.tl/BlairGMO
    CBC, 'GM foods not served in Monsanto cafeteria', 22 Dec 1999, nin.tl/
Monsantocafe

35 P Tyson, 'Should we grow GM crops?' PBS, 1999,
pbs.org/wgbh/harvest/exist/

36 EUR-LEX, 'Regulation (EC) No 1829/2003 of the European Parliament
and of the Council of 22 Sep 2003 on genetically modified food and feed
(Text with EEA relevance)', nin.tl/EURLex

37 C Fernandez, 'Most meat tainted by GM', *Daily Mail*, 24 Feb 2016, nin.tl/
GMmeatUK

38 House of Commons Science and Technology Committee,
'Bioengineering', Seventh Report of Session 2009-10, HC 220, 25 Mar
2010, p 34, nin.tl/bioengineering

39 BBC News Online, 'GM 'golden rice' opponents wicked, says minister
Owen Paterson', 14 Oct 2013, bbc.co.uk/news/uk-politics-24515938
    Bill and Melinda Gates Foundation, 'Agricultural Development: Golden
Rice', no date, nin.tl/goldenrice

40 National Chicken Council, 'Broiler Chicken Industry Key Facts 2016',
nin.tl/broilerfacts
    National Geographic, 'Thanksgiving Day Facts: Pilgrims, Dinner,
Parades, More', 24 Nov 2009, nin.tl/Thanksgiving
    JJ McGlone, 'Transport of Market Pigs: Improvements in Welfare and
Economics' in Temple Grandin (ed.), *Livestock Handling and Transport,
4th Edition: Theories and Applications*, CABI, p. 298.
    North American Meat Institute, 'The United States Meat Industry at a
Glance', 2013, nin.tl/meatglance
    DR Simon, 2013, *Meatonomics*, Conari Press, pp 248, note 44.

41 M Zaraska, 'This is why you crave beef', *Salon*, 3 Apr 2016, nin.tl/cravebeef

42 Ibid.

43 R Johnson, op cit.

44 Ibid.

45 Ibid.

46 Ibid.

47 The Humane Society of the United States, 'Welfare Issues with the Use
of Hormones and Antibiotics in Animal Agriculture', 2016. *AGRIBUSINESS*,
33, nin.tl/humane

48 Ibid.

49 Ibid.

50 Ibid.

51 Ibid.
52 Associated Press, 'California adopts strict limits on livestock antibiotics', 10 Oct 2015.
53 ER Gold & J Carbone, 'Myriad Genetics', *Genetics in Medicine*, 2010, no 12, pp 39-70.
    CS Chuang & DT Lau, 'Patenting Human Genes', *Clinical Therapeutics*, 32(12), 2010, p 2054.
54 Bernice Schacter, *Issues and Dilemmas of Biotechnology*, Greenwood Press, 1999, pp 25-36.
    World Intellectual Property Organization, 'Bioethics and Patent Law', *WIPO Magazine*, Sep 2006, nin.tl/WIPO
55 Juan He, 'Developing Countries' Pursuit of an Intellectual Property Law Balance under the WTO TRIPS Agreement', *Chinese Journal of International Law*, Nov 2011.
56 AR Chapman, 'The Human Rights Implications of Intellectual Property Protection', *Journal of International Economic Law*, 5(4), 2002, pp 861-82.
57 WW Fisher & CP Rigamonti, 'The South Africa AIDS Controversy', *The Law and Business Patents*, 10 Feb 2005, pp 1-56, nin.tl/AIDSrow
58 CM Correa, 'Bilateralism in Intellectual Property', *Case Western Reserve Journal of International Law*, 36(1), 2004, pp 79-95.
59 Declaration of Joseph E Stiglitz, US District Court for the Southern District of New York, Case 1:09-cv-04515-RWS, Document 224, File 01/20/2010, Civil Action No. 09-4515 (RWS), pp 1-6, nin.tl/Stiglitz
60 Ibid.
61 TPP, 'Chapter 18: Intellectual Property, Section A: General Provisions', nin.tl/TPPchap18
    On the Philippines, for example, consider the following: 'The Philippines pharmaceutical market is projected to reach US$1.4 billion in 2008, equal to nearly US$15 per capita. In terms of the overall market, this is comparable to the market size of Thailand. The Philippine pharmaceutical market is highly dependent on import of raw materials to manufacture drugs. About 95% of the materials compounded in the territory are imported, and the industry is concentrated on manufacturing products discovered and developed elsewhere. Compared to other more developed territories that have established themselves in the formulation of breakthrough pharmaceutical products, innovation and discovery of drugs in the territory is relatively small business.' Source: PricewaterhouseCooper, 'The changing dynamics of pharma outsourcing in Asia', 2008, p 46, nin.tl/pharmaoutsource
62 TPP, op cit.

9 Financialization: 'A highway without speed limits'

1 See my books *The Great Brexit Swindle*, Clairview Books, 2016 and *President Trump, Inc*, Clairview Books, 2017.
2 P Navarro and W Ross, 'Scoring the Trump Economic Plan', 29 Sep 2016, nin.tl/Navarro
3 Greenpeace Netherlands, 'TTIP Leaks', no date, ttip-leaks.org

Trade in Services Agreement, draft texts, wikileaks.org/tisa

4 C Goodhart and D Schoenmaker, 'The United States dominates global investment banking: does it matter for Europe?', LSE Financial Markets Group Paper Series, Mar 2016, Special Paper 243,

5 Ibid.

6 J Hensarling, 'Too Big to Jail', 11 July 2016, 114th Congress, nin.tl/Hensarling

The report says: 'Because DOJ [Department of Justice] failed to comply or even produce a single page of responsive records in more than two years, the Committee authorized and issued a subpoena *duces tecum* [a subpoena for the production of evidence] on May 11 2015, compelling Attorney General Lynch to produce the long-requested records [specific to HSBC] by not later than May 25 2015. Notwithstanding the Committee's multiple requests for this information, and a congressional subpoena requiring Attorney General Lynch to timely produce it to the Committee, DOJ to date has failed to produce any records pertaining to its prosecutorial decision making with respect to HSBC or any large financial institution and has not provided a legal basis that might reasonably justify its actions. Consequently, Attorney General Lynch remains in default on her legal obligation to produce the subpoenaed records to the Committee' (p 28).

7 Financial Crisis Inquiry Commission, 'Final Report of the National Commission on the Causes of the Financial and Economic Crisis in the United States', Jan 2011, nin.tl/CrisisInquiry

On Bush, see SG Stolberg, 'A private, blunter Bush declares, "Wall Street got drunk"', *New York Times*, 23 July 2008, nin.tl/Drunk

8 Financial Crisis Inquiry Commission, op cit. Multibillionaire CEO Warren Buffett warned investors years before the crisis of 2008 that: 'The rapidly growing trade in derivatives poses a "mega-catastrophic risk" for the economy and most shares are still "too expensive"'. BBC News Online, 'Buffett warns on investment 'time bomb', 4 Mar 2003, nin.tl/Buffett

9 Financial Crisis Inquiry, op cit.

C Isidore, '35 bankers were sent to prison for financial crisis crimes', CNN Money, 28 Apr 2016.

H Kuchler, D Schaefer & J Pickard, 'Financial crisis just a 'blip' for bankers', *Financial Times*, 21 Feb 2013, nin.tl/blip

10 PricewaterhouseCoopers, 'Driving business growth in 2016', 2016, nin.tl/PWC2016

Editorial Board, 'Why should taxpayers give big banks $83 billion a year?' Bloomberg, 20 Feb 2013, nin.tl/Bloomberg2013

11 PD Culpepper & R Reinke, 'Structural Power and Bank Bailouts in the United Kingdom and the United States', *Politics and Society*, Sep 2014, doi: 10.1177/0032329214547342

E Conway, 'RBS and Lloyds nationalised in all but name, says Bank of England Governor Mervyn King', *Telegraph*, 26 Feb 2009, nin.tl/King

12 Culpepper & Reinke, op cit.

13 Ibid.

14 Ibid.

15 BBC News Online, 'Eurozone debt web: Who owes what to whom?' 18 Nov 2011, nin.tl/debtweb

16 L Puccio, 'TTIP and regulation of financial markets', European Parliamentary Research Service, June 2015, nin.tl/Puccio

17 S George, 'Getting away with murder', *New Internationalist*, 1 May 2015, nin.tl/George

    J Hopkin, 'Technocrats have taken over governments in Southern Europe', LSE, 24 Apr 2014, nin.tl/Hopkin

    Hopkin says that it isn't all bad: 'After nearly four months of technocratic government in Italy, a more nuanced picture is emerging. First of all, early optimism that Italy could begin to roll over its large public debt more cheaply has run into the stark reality that European financial operators have essentially lost faith in Southern European sovereign debt, due to fears about the feasibility of the austerity and reform package. Put simply, the official position of the European Commission and Central Bank remains that distressed periphery economies all need to simultaneously undergo an economic adjustment that many economists believe is impossible (they must rebalance both very large current account deficits and very large public deficits in a context of zero and possibly negative nominal GDP growth)'.

18 J Pietras, 'Austerity measures in the EU', European Institute, nin.tl/Pietras

19 Oxfam, 'A cautionary tale', Oxfam Briefing Paper, 174, Sep 2013, nin.tl/cautionary

    A Kapur, N Macleod & N Singh, 'Plutonomy: Buying Luxury, Explaining Global Imbalances', Equity Strategy, Citigroup, 16 Oct 2005.

    Kapur et al, 'Revisiting Plutonomy', Equity Strategy, Citigroup, 5 Mar 2006.

    L Martin & J Garnett, 1997, *British Foreign Policy: Challenges and Choices for the 21st Century*, Pinter.

20 For example, the UN Economic and Social Council states: 'The adoption of fiscal consolidation programmes may be necessary for the implementation of economic and social rights. If such programmes are not implemented with full respect for human rights standards and do not take into account the obligations of States towards the rights holders, however, they may adversely affect a range of rights protected by the International Covenant on Economic, Social and Cultural Rights. Most at risk are labour rights, including the right to work (art. 6), the right to just and favourable conditions of work, including the right to fair wages and to a minimum wage that provides workers with a decent living for themselves and their families (art. 7), the right to collective bargaining (art. 8), the right to social security, including unemployment benefits, social assistance and old-age pensions (arts. 9 and 11), the right to an adequate standard of living, including the right to food and the right to housing (art. 11), the right to health and access to adequate health care (art. 12) and the right to education (arts. 13-14). Low-income families, especially those with children, and workers with the lowest qualifications are disproportionately affected by measures such as job cuts, minimum wage freezes and cutbacks in social assistance benefits, which potentially result in discrimination on the grounds of social origin or

property (art. 2 (2)). Moreover, reductions in the levels of public services or the introduction of or increase in user fees in areas such as childcare, and preschool education, public utilities and family support services have a disproportionate impact on women, and thus may amount to a step backwards in terms of gender equality (arts. 3 and 10)'. Source: UNESCO, Committee on Economic, Social and Cultural Rights, 'Public debt, austerity measures and the International Covenant on Economic, Social and Cultural Rights', E/C.12/2016/1, 22 July 2016, nin.tl/UNESC

M Kremer & S Jayachandran, 'Odious Debt', *Finance and Development*, June 2002, 39(2), nin.tl/Kremer

Referring to so-called developing countries, not specifically Europe, Kremer and Jayachandran write: 'Under the law in many countries, individuals do not have to repay if others fraudulently borrow in their name, and corporations are not liable for contracts that their chief executive officers or other agents enter into without the authority to bind the corporations. The legal doctrine of odious debt makes an analogous argument that sovereign debt incurred without the consent of the people and not benefiting the people is odious and should not be transferable to a successor government, especially if creditors are aware of these facts in advance.'

21 Corporate Europe Observatory, 'The European Stability Mechanism (ESM', 5 June 2014, nin.tl/ESM

S George, 'State of Corporations: The rise of illegitimate power and the threat to democracy' in *State of Power 2014: Exposing the Davos Class*, Transnational Institute and Occupy.com (eds), 2014, pp 8-15, nin.tl/GeorgeTNI

KA Janse, 'How the financial crisis made Europe stronger', World Economic Forum, 16 Mar, 2016, nin.tl/Janse

22 Janse, op cit, and UNICEF, '2.6 million more children plunged into poverty in rich countries during Great Recession', 28 Oct 2014, unicef.org/media/media_76447.html

22 L Puccio, op cit.

24 AMCHAM EU et al, Letter to Mr Karel De Gucht and Mr Michael Froman, 16 Nov 2011, nin.tl/AMCHAM

25 European Commission, 'Textual Proposal: Possible Provisions on State Enterprises and Enterprises Granted Special or Exclusive Rights or Privileges', Jan 2015, nin.tl/EC2015

European Commission, 'Textual Proposal: Possible Provision on Subsidies', Jan 2015, nin.tl/EC2015-2

26 D Rodrik, 'The muddled case for trade agreements', Project Syndicate, 13 July 2015, nin.tl/Rodrik

27 Ibid, and Martin & Garnett, op cit.

28 TTIP, 'Trade in Services and Investment Schedule of Specific Commitments and Reservations', 2014, nin.tl/TTIPBBC2015

S Naugès & T Forbin, 'French Decree Extends List of Foreign Investments That Must Obtain Prior Authorisation', *McDermott Will and Emery*, 23 May 2014, nin.tl/MWE

29 D Mekouar, 'These Are America's Richest & Poorest States', *Voice of*

America, 21 Sep 2015, nin.tl/Mekouar
  European Commission, 'Public procurement in TTIP', Jan 2015, nin.tl/ECTTIP

30 GATS Article 2(a) of the Annex on Financial Services, nin.tl/GATS2a

31 European Banking Federation, 'Financial regulatory chapter and ISDS in TTIP', EBF_010590, 27 Jan 2015, nin.tl/EBF2015.

32 Ibid and British Government, 'Financial Services and TTIP', no date, nin.tl/UKgovTTIP
  British Government, 'Insurance Services and TTIP', nin.tl/TTIPinsurance

33 Ibid.

34 European Commission, 'EU-US Transatlantic Trade and Investment Partnership (TTIP): Cooperation on financial services regulation', Jan 2014, nin.tl/ECTTIP2014

35 M Rake, 'CBI President Speech to CBI Annual Dinner 2015', 20 May 2015, nin.tl/Rake

36 Lloyds, 'Trade negotiations', no date, nin.tl/Lloyds

37 T Stephenson, 'Transatlantic Trade & Investment Partnership (TTIP) – What it might mean for the insurance sector', Robus, 19 Jan 2015, nin.tl/Robus

38 K Alexander, 'The GATS and Financial Servicess' in K Alexander & M Andenas (eds), *The World Trade Organization and Trade in Services*, Martinus Nijhoff, 2008, p 573.
  RJ Ahearn & IF Fergusson, 'World Trade Organization (WTO): Issues in the Debate on Continued US Participation', Congressional Research Service, 16 June 2010, p 7.

39 Insurance Europe, 'Position paper for the TTIP', 12 Dec 2014, nin.tl/InsuranceEurope

40 Ibid.

41 Association of German Banks, 'Enhanced Prudential Standards and Early Remediation Requirements for Foreign Banking Organizations and Foreign Non-bank Financial Companies; Docket no. R-1438 and RIN 7100-AD-86', letter to Robert deV Frierson (Secretary, Board of Governors of the Federal Reserve System), May 2013, nin.tl/AGB

42 Ibid.

43 ibid.

44 European Banking Federation, 'financial regulatory chapter and isds in TTIP', EBF_010590, 27 Jan 2015, ebf-fbe.eu and AGB, op cit..

45 D Vincenti, 'TTIP will not include financial services, says US ambassador', EurActiv, 16 July 2014, nin.tl/Vincenti

46 European Commission, 'Trade in Services, Investment and E-Commerce: Chapter II –Investment', Sep 2015, nin.tl/ECtrade2015

10 Healthcare: 'Selling splints to Europe'

1 EC Schneider, DO Sarnak, D Squires, A Shah and MM Doty, 'Mirror, Mirror 2017: International Comparison Reflects Flaws and Opportunities for Better US Health Care', July 2017, nin.tl/mirror
  W Martin, 'The 16 countries with the world's best healthcare systems', *Business Insider* (UK), 13 Jan 2013, nin.tl/prosperity

2 EB Solomont, 'Doctors: Insurance Companies Affect Treatment', *New York Sun*, 15 Sep 2008, nin.tl/Solomont

3 L Girion, 'Insurers refuse to limit policy cancellations', *LA Times*, 17 June 2009. nin.tl/cancellations

4 S Kirchgaessner, 'Half a Million Americans Denied Health Coverage', *Financial Times*, 13 Oct 2010, nin.tl/coverage

5 Cecilia Malmström letter to Lord Livingston, Minister of State for Trade and Investment, UK, 26 Jan 2016, nin.tl/Malmstrom
   An example of a private finance initiative (PFI) is a government scheme to contract a private company to build a hospital with taxpayers' money. This scheme was introduced under John Major's Conservative government in 1992 and expanded markedly under Tony Blair's New Labour regime. By 2015, the NHS was spending £3,700 ($4,800) per minute to pay for the privately financed hospitals, according to the *Telegraph*. 'Bills have grown so large they would pay for the wages of all qualified midwives for two and half years.' Source: R Mendick, L Donnelly & A Kirk, 'The PFI hospitals costing NHS £2bn every year', *Telegraph*, 18 July 2015, nin.tl/PFIhospitals
   Between 2012 and 2017, taxpayers forked out £300 billion ($388bn) to pay for 717 PFI contracts, according to a *Guardian* projection. Source: D Campbell, J Ball & S Rogers, 'PFI will ultimately cost £300bn', *Guardian*, 5 July 2012, nin.tl/PFIcost

6 DGUV and SVLFG (German Government and Sozialversicherung für Landwirtschaft, Forsten und Gartenbau), 'Comments by the statutory accident insurance institutions in Germany on a Transatlantic Trade and Investment Partnership (TTIP) between the European Union and the USA', 2014, nin.tl/DGUV
   On expensive medical equipment, to which few can afford access in the US, see G Ridic, S Gleason & O Ridic, 'Comparisons of Health Care Systems in the United States, Germany and Canada', *Materia Socio Medica*, 2012, 24(2), pp 112-120. They write: 'In 1997 Canada's 53 MRIs meant one for every 572,000 citizens (contrast that figure to 2046 MRIs in the US, one for every 130,800 Americans). Access to open heart surgery and organ transplantation is also restricted. That same year the 245 CT scanners in Canada meant one for every 123,500 citizens. The United States had 3667 CT scanners, one for every 73,000 Americans. Recent studies found Canadian deficits in several areas including angioplasty, cardiac catheterization and intensive care. Waiting lists for certain surgical and diagnostic procedures are common in Canada. Nationwide, the average wait for treatment is 13.3 weeks. The average waiting time in more than 80 per cent of the procedures is one third longer than Canadian physicians consider clinically reasonable.'

7 Ridic et al, op. cit.

8 PV Dutton, 'Health care in France and the United States', Brookings Institution, July 2002, nin.tl/Dutton

9 Ibid.

10 National Bureau of Economic Statistics, 'Comparing the US and Canadian Health Care Systems', no date, nin.tl/comparing

R Blizzard, 'Healthcare System Ratings: US, Great Britain, Canada', Gallup, 25 Mar 2003, nin.tl/Gallup

11 S Eger & JC Mahlich, 'Pharmaceutical regulation in Europe and its impact on corporate R&D', *Health Economics Review*, 2014, 4(23), DOI: 10.1186/s13561-014-0023-5.

E Rome, 'Big Pharma Pockets $711 Billion in Profits by Robbing Seniors, Taxpayers', Huffington Post, 8 Apr 2013, nin.tl/robseniors

12 nin.tl/breakout

13 E Whitman, 'How the US subsidizes cheap drugs For Europe', *International Business Times*, 24 Sep 2015, nin.tl/subsidizing

14 Ibid and Rome, op cit.

15 W Beveridge, 'Social Insurance and Allied Services', Nov 1942, nin.tl/Beveridge

16 Ibid.

17 W Churchill, 'Mr Churchill's Declaration of Policy to the Electors', nin.tl/Churchill2

J Lister, *Cutting the Lifeline: The Fight for the NHS*, 1988, Journeyman, p 36.

18 House of Commons Treasury Committee, 'Private Finance Initiative', 17th Report of Session 2010-12, Vol I, HC 1146, Aug 2011, nin.tl/PFI2

The report notes that the 'majority of PFI debt still does not appear in government debt or deficit figures' (p 3).

I Newman, 2014, *Reclaiming Local Democracy*, Policy Press, p 31.

Newman writes: 'In 1992, the Conservatives introduced the [PFI]... The scheme was implemented in health and transport but only one local authority signed a PFI scheme under the Conservatives. In total, 34, PFI schemes were agreed in the 10 years between 1986 and 1996, worth £2 billion [$2.6bn]. New Labour revamped the scheme and in the following 10 years (1996-2006), 549 PFI schemes were agreed, worth £51 billion [$66bn], including many local authority PFI schemes. Over £260 billion [$336.5bn] in PFI commitments were accrued by the time Labour left office, for buildings valued at around £60 billion [$77.6bn].'

19 Consultancy.uk, 'Global healthcare consulting market grows to 6.3 billion', 19 Jan 2015, nin.tl/consulting

National Institute for Health Research, 'Do management consultants improve the quality of NHS commissioning', 5 Mar 2015, nin.tl/consultants

Department of Health, *Equity and excellence: Liberating the NHS*, July 2010, Cm 7881, nin.tl/NHS2010

This White Paper states: 'Our ambition is to create the largest and most vibrant social enterprise sector in the world. The Government's intention is to free foundation trusts from constraints they are under', meaning they want to deregulate, 'in line with their original conception, so they can innovate to improve care for patients'. Innovation means looking for ways to cope in the absence of funding. 'In future, they will be regulated in the same way as any other providers, whether from the private or voluntary sector' (p 36).

20 Department of Health, op cit.

21 Apax, 'Opportunities Post Global Healthcare Reforms', Oct 2010, nin.tl/
    Apax
22 Ibid.
23 D Rose, 'The firm that hijacked the NHS', *Daily Mail*, 12 Feb 2012, nin.tl/
    Lansley
24 US Chamber of Commerce, 'Face of Trade: Selling Splints to Europe',
    no date, nin.tl/sellingsplints
25 CarterSchwartz, 'NHS outsourcing attracting wave of health investors
    from across the Pond', 10 Feb 2016, nin.tl/outsourcing
26 B Borland, 'NHS Scotland in takeover by US health giant', *Express*, 22 Feb
    2010, nin.tl/Borland
27 P Gallagher, 'Is Simon Stevens really the right person to run the NHS?',
    Independent, 24 Oct 2013, nin.tl/Stevens
28 Quoted in PV Dutton, 2007, *Differential Diagnoses*, ILR Press (Cornell
    University Press), p 169.
29 EM Melhado, 'Health Planning in the United States and the Decline
    of Public-interest Policymaking', *Milbank Quarterly*, June 2006, 84(2),
    pp 359–440.
       A Brimelow, 'Could US health firm hold key to NHS reform?' BBC News
    Online, 18 May 2010, nin.tl/Brimelow
30 D Light, 'Making the NHS more like Kaiser Permanente', BMJ, 2004,
    Vol 328, p 763.
31 L Donnelly, 'Hospital records of all NHS patients sold to insurers',
    Telegraph, 23 Feb 2014, nin.tl/patientssold
       Dutton, op cit.
       L Presser, M Hruskova, H Rowbottom & J Kancir, 'Care.data and access
    to UK health records', *Journal of Technology and Science*, 8 Nov 2015,
    techscience.org/a/2015081103/
32 Presser et al, op cit.
33 Ibid.
34 TTIP, 'Cross-Border Trade in Services in Text Consolidation [draft]',
    30 Nov 2015, ttip-leaks.org/menelaos/doc3.pdf
       TISA, 'Annex on Government Procurement', Apr 2015, nin.tl/
    wikileaksTISA
35 TTIP, 'Electronic Communications/Telecommunications Text [draft]', no
    date, nin.tl/TTIPleak
36 TISA, 'Annex on Telecommunications Services [draft]', no date, nin.tl/
    TISAleak2
37 R Moore-Colyer, 'IBM modernises NHS electronic staff record system
    with mobile access', v3, 26 Mar 2015, nin.tl/IBM
38 R Daws, 'Spectralink Interview', TelecomsTech, 10 Feb 2014, nin.tl/Daws
       Polycom, 'National Health Service (NHS)', no date, nin.tl/Polycom
39 *New Scientist*, 'Revealed: Google AI has access to huge haul of NHS
    patient data', 29 Apr 2016, nin.tl/GoogleAI

INDEX

For acronyms see list on pp7–9.